"Okie Ghosts a

Chapter 1:

The Great Squirrel Siege Parade Float Fiasco

The first Saturday in June always started hotter than a stolen tamale in Weatherford, Oklahoma, and this year was no different. By nine a.m., the sun was already scorching the asphalt on Airport Road as if it held a personal grudge. Out in front of the Hargrove family farm, around two hundred locals—more or less those mainly there for the free watermelon—gathered around what was supposed to be the grand marshal float for the annual Pa's Folly Festival.

What it actually looked like was a rusted flatbed trailer hauled by Junior's 1978 Ford pickup, decorated with chicken wire, duct tape, and roughly four thousand fake acorns spray-painted gold. Sitting atop this setup was a twelve-foot-tall plywood squirrel wearing a Confederate kepi and wielding a toilet-plunger bayonet. The squirrel's beady eyes—two busted taillights from a '92 Chevy—glinted with malevolent intent. Painted across the side of the trailer in dripping red letters were the words: "IN LOVING MEMORY OF EARL HARGROVE'S GREAT SQUIRREL SIEGE OF '98."

Maude Hargrove, sixty-eight years young and tougher than overcooked jerky, stood on the porch steps in her starched denim dress, arms crossed, watching the disaster unfold with the weary expression of a woman who'd seen this exact brand of nonsense for forty-five years running.
"Billy," she hollered, voice cutting through the bluegrass band warming up in the yard, "you sure that contraption ain't gonna kill somebody this year?"
Billy, the eldest son, popped out from behind the float like a manic jack-in-the-box. His hair stuck up in sweat-plastered spikes, and his eyes had that telltale glitter—the one that meant he was three days into a high and convinced he was Leonardo da Vinci reincarnated as a welder.

"Ma, relax! I reinforced the launch mechanism with aircraft-grade baling wire. Thing's safer than a church raffle!"

He proudly patted what looked like a homemade catapult bolted to the trailer bed. It was loaded with burlap sacks labeled "ACORN BOMBS." The plan—Billy had explained it seventeen times—was for the catapult to fling the sacks into the crowd during the parade, where they would burst open in a glorious shower of foam acorns, delighting children and commemorating Earl's legendary war on the backyard squirrels.

Darla Sue, the middle child and only one with a lick of common sense, leaned against the porch railing, sipping iced tea so sweet it could strip paint. "Billy, the only thing that catapult's gonna launch is you into a lawsuit when one of those sacks takes out Mrs. Potts's glass eye."

Reverend Potts, standing nearby in his seersucker suit, clutched his Bible tighter. "The good Lord gave us dominion over the beasts, not artillery."

Junior, the youngest and laziest, lounged in the bed of his pickup eating a MoonPie and filming everything on his phone for the festival's TikTok account. "Y'all hush. This is content."

Little Zeke, twelve going on feral, scampered up the ladder to the squirrel's shoulders and wedged himself inside the hollow plywood torso. "I'm the general!" he yelled, voice echoing tinnily. "Squirrels never surrender!"

Maude pinched the bridge of her nose. "Earl, if you're up there watchin', I swear on your rusty urn I'm gonna dig you up and scatter you in the septic tank."

The parade was set to start in ten minutes. The high school marching band struck up a wobbly version of "Rocky Top." Billy climbed onto the trailer, gave the crowd a double thumb-up, and yanked the catapult's release cord with theatrical flair.

Nothing happened.

He yanked harder.

Still nothing.

"Little sticky," he muttered, then threw his full 220 pounds into it.

The cord snapped free with a sound like a banjo string breaking. The catapult arm whipped forward at Mach Jesus, launching not just the burlap sacks but the entire counterweight—a stack of cinder blocks Billy had "borrowed" from the Baptist church's new fellowship hall.

The cinder blocks sailed in a perfect arc, smashed through the windshield of Reverend Potts's parked Buick, and kept going until they landed square in the prize watermelon patch. Twenty-three ripe melons exploded in a pink mist that rained down like a biblical plague.

At the exact same moment, the recoil snapped the catapult's base clean off the trailer. The whole apparatus toppled sideways, slamming into the giant plywood squirrel. The squirrel teetered, groaned, and—because nothing in the Hargrove family ever failed small—collapsed directly onto Billy.

For one frozen second, the crowd stared at a twelve-foot Confederate squirrel pinning Billy Hargrove to the flatbed while foam acorns trickled out like sad confetti.

Then Zeke's muffled voice echoed from inside the wreckage: "We surrender! We surrender!"

Darla Sue spit sweet tea out her nose. Junior howled with laughter, phone still recording. Maude just sighed, walked down the steps, and poked the squirrel's leg with her boot.

"Billy, you alive under there?"

A weak thumb-up emerged from beneath the plywood.

"Good," Maude said. "Because you're payin' for them watermelons and the Reverend's windshield. And if that fool squirrel crushed your spine, I ain't wheeling you around till Christmas."

The marching band, God bless 'em, kept playing "Rocky Top" like professionals. A couple of teenagers started clapping. Someone yelled, "Best float yet!"

Maude looked heavenward again. "Earl, you happy now? Your idiot children are still tryin' to outdumb you."

From somewhere in the distance—or maybe just the heat shimmer off the hood of Junior's truck—came the faintest sound of maniacal laughter.

The Pa's Folly Festival had officially begun.

Chapter 2:

Earl's Drive-Thru Chapel of Holy Matrimony (and Divorce on Demand)

Maude Hargrove stood in the middle of the yard, hands on hips, surveying the smoking remains of the squirrel float like a general inspecting a battlefield. Firemen were still hosing down stray foam acorns that had caught fire—nobody knew how—and Reverend Potts kept fanning himself with his Bible, muttering about signs and portents.

Darla Sue poked the taxidermied armadillo on the porch rocker with the toe of her sandal. The thing had been sitting there since Earl's funeral, wearing a tiny straw cowboy hat and holding a sign that read "WILL BITE FOR BEER." Something inside it rattled again, like marbles in a tin can.

"Ma," Darla called, "why is Pa's stuffed varmint making noises? You been feedin' it after midnight?"

Maude waved a dismissive hand. "Your daddy stuffed that thing himself during one of his lows. Probably just rocks for ballast. Or loose teeth. Hard to say."

Reverend Potts edged closer, face the color of expired milk. "Sister Maude, I don't mean to speak ill of the dead, but that float… that squirrel… it was downright pagan. How did Earl ever come up with such foolishness?"

Maude took a long, deliberate sip of her sweet tea, ice clinking like judgment day. Then she fixed the reverend with a stare sharp enough to skin a cat.

"Pagan? Reverend, you want pagan. Let me tell you about the summer of 2003, when Earl decided the barn wasn't pullin' its weight and turned it into the Hargrove Holy Roller Wedding Chapel and 24-Hour Divorce Corral. That was pagan. With a drive-thru."

The reverend's eyebrows shot up so fast they nearly took flight. Junior stopped filming long enough to grin. Billy, still half-buried under plywood, gave a muffled whoop of recognition. Even the firemen paused their hosing to listen—everybody in Weatherford knew the legend, but Maude's version was the gold standard.

It started, Maude said, on a Tuesday in June when the heat index hit 112, and Earl hadn't slept in four days straight. Classic high. Eyes wild, talking a mile a minute, convinced he'd cracked the code to easy money and spiritual salvation all in one go.

He marched into the kitchen at dawn wearing nothing but boxer shorts and welding goggles, waving a hand-drawn blueprint the size of a tablecloth. "Maude, baby, I have seen the future! People don't want fancy churches and expensive preachers. They want convenience. Like Sonic, but for matrimony!"

Maude, flipping bacon at the stove, didn't even look up. "Earl, the only thing you're seein' is the inside of your own eyelids if you don't get some sleep."
But sleep was for mortals. By Wednesday night, Earl had sawed a giant window into the barn door big enough for a pickup truck to drive through. By

Thursday, he'd welded together a neon sign out of old Coors lights and Christmas bulbs that flickered "I DO… OR I DON'T (NO JUDGMENT)." It shorted out every hour on the hour and sometimes read "I DO… NOT."

Friday, he raided the closet for his white Elvis jumpsuit—the one with the eagle collar he'd bought off eBay after watching Viva Las Vegas one too many times. Saturday morning, he declared the grand opening.

Word spread faster than chiggers in July. By noon, a line of vehicles stretched down the county road: rusty pickups, one motorcycle with a sidecar, and a bewildered couple in a U-Haul who thought it was a shortcut.

Earl stood at the drive-thru window in full Elvis regalia, pompadour slicked to high heaven, holding a cordless karaoke microphone hooked to a boom box blasting "Love Me Tender."

"Welcome to holy matrimony, drive-thru style! Pull forward, state your intentions, and keep your hands on the wheel at all times!"

The first customers were Tommy Ray Jenkins and his high school sweetheart, Kayla Dawn, who'd been engaged since prom and wanted something quick before he shipped out to basic training. They pulled up in Tommy's jacked-up Chevy, tin cans already rattling from the bumper.

Earl leaned out the window like a carhop on uppers. "Do you, Tommy Ray, take this woman to have and to hold, in sickness and health, till death or trade-in do you part?"

Tommy Ray, sweating bullets, yelled, "I do!"

"And do you, Kayla Dawn, take this man, for better or worse, richer or poorer, as long as the truck payments last?"

Kayla giggled. "I do!"

"By the power vested in me by the internet and the state of Oklahoma—probably—I now pronounce you hitched. Kiss the bride, tip the preacher, and pull forward for your complimentary scuppernong wine!"

It was going smooth as greased bacon until Kayla's daddy, Big Hank Pritchard, showed up waving a shotgun and roaring that Tommy Ray wasn't good enough for his little girl.

Tommy floored it. The truck lurched forward, dragging tin cans and Earl—who'd grabbed the bumper for a "blessing sprint"—ten yards before he let go and rolled into the ditch like a rhinestone tumbleweed.

That should've been the end of it, but Earl was just getting warmed up.
Next, he installed what he called the "Holy Smoke of Sanctification"—an old mosquito fogger filled with dollar-store incense. During the third ceremony, the fogger went haywire and pumped the barn so full of

smoke that nobody could see their own vows. When the haze cleared, two couples had accidentally swapped partners. One bride was kissing the best man. The groom was signing the certificate with a Sharpie that bled through three pages.

Then came the ring-bearer chickens.

Earl had dressed two Rhode Island Reds in tiny bow ties and trained them—sort of—to waddle down the aisle with rings tied to their legs. They made it halfway before deciding freedom tasted better than matrimony. The chase that followed involved six groomsmen, one angry goose that wandered in off the pond, and Earl swinging a butterfly net while singing "Can't Help Falling in Love."

The unity candle got knocked over. Hay bales caught fire. Somebody opened the barn doors for ventilation, and the chickens escaped into the parking lot, leading half the wedding party on a merry chase through rows of pickup trucks.

By sunset, the fire department had been called twice, three annulments had already been requested in the hayloft "divorce corral," and Earl was trying to livestream the whole thing on dial-up internet using a webcam duct-taped to a ceiling fan.

The feed froze forever on a bride named Tiffany saying "I—" while her groom peeled out in reverse, tin cans clattering like applause.

Maude finished her story just as the last fireman rolled up his hose. The yard smelled like burnt foam, incense, and watermelon carnage.
Reverend Potts looked faint. "And the Lord allowed this… abomination to continue?"

Maude shrugged. "Lasted six weeks. Made enough money to pay the property taxes and buy me a new washer. Then the health department shut him down for 'unsanitary poultry practices.' Earl spent the next month in the bunker writing sad country songs about lost love and chicken betrayal."

Junior, still filming, zoomed in on the taxidermied armadillo. "Best summer ever."

Darla Sue picked up the armadillo and gave it a shake. The rattle sounded louder this time—definitely not rocks.

"Ma," she said slowly, "I think Pa hid something in here. Something papery."

Maude's eyes narrowed. "Well, don't just stand there shakin' it like a maraca. Get my Phillips head and a trash bag. If it's another one of his 'treasures,' I want witnesses."

As Darla headed for the toolbox, a hot wind swept through the yard, rattling the neon beer signs on the porch and sending a single foam acorn tumbling across the grass like a tiny ghost.

Somewhere in the distance—or maybe just in Maude's imagination—Earl's laugh echoed one more time.

The festival had barely started, and the real folly was just getting underway.

Chapter 3:

Bunker Blues and the Armadillo's Last Laugh

Darla Sue cradled the taxidermied armadillo as it might bite her—or worse, quote Earl's poetry. The little bandit's glassy eyes stared up with eternal judgment, straw cowboy hat tilted at a rakish angle that said, "I've seen things." She gave it a suspicious third shake. Whatever was inside didn't just rattle—it clattered, clinked, and ended with a suspicious thunk like something heavy shifting.

"Ma," Darla announced to the porch audience, "this thing's either got Pa's will, a mason jar of moonshine, or a live grenade he forgot to pull the pin on in '98."

Junior's phone was already up, red record light blinking. "Please be the grenade. Views would go nuclear."

Billy, still dusty from his squirrel-pinning, hobbled over on one good leg and one that was rapidly swelling like rising biscuit dough. "Gimme that varmint! If it's Pa's secret flux-capacitor plans, I'm buildin' it first!"

He lunged. Darla yanked the armadillo out of reach. Billy's momentum carried him forward, straight into Reverend Potts, who was still clutching his Bible like a life raft. The collision sent the reverend staggering backward into the porch swing, which—thanks to years of dry rot—promptly collapsed. Potts landed flat on his back in the wreckage, legs in the air, Bible flying open to a random page that landed upside-down on his face like a holy paper bag.

"Sweet mercy!" the reverend yelped, muffled by Leviticus.

Zeke, never one to miss chaos, darted in to "help" by trying to pull the Bible off. Instead, he grabbed the reverend's toupee—nobody had known it was a toupee until that exact moment—and yanked. The hairpiece came off with a Velcro rip, revealing a shiny dome that reflected the noon sun like a signal mirror.

The crowd—firemen, neighbors, and one confused UPS guy who'd picked the wrong day to deliver—erupted in gasps, then barely-stifled snickers.

Maude didn't flinch. She just marched over, snatched the toupee from Zeke's hand, and slapped it back on the reverend's head backward. "There. Good as new. Now quit floppin' around like a catfish on a dock." Potts sat up, toupee now resembling a dead possum riding reverse, and tried to regain dignity. "The Lord tests us in mysterious ways."

"Lord's got nothin' on Earl," Maude muttered.

She turned to Darla. "Hand it over before these clowns turn it into a football."

Darla complied. Maude flipped the armadillo belly-up on the picnic table with the ceremony of a bomb tech. Its stiff little legs pointed skyward like it was surrendering to fate. She jammed her Phillips-head into the seam Earl had stitched with 50-pound fishing line.

First twist: nothing.

Second twist: a thread popped and a moth the size of a hummingbird exploded out, did one confused loop, and dive-bombed straight into Billy's open mouth.

She pulled it out. The armadillo, suddenly lighter, rolled off the table, bounced off Billy's swollen ankle (eliciting a howl), and landed upright on the porch floor, staring at everyone like it had planned the whole thing.

Darla untied the ribbon and unrolled the papers. The top sheet was in Earl's unmistakable scrawl: "Last Will and Testament of Earl Theodore Hargrove – For My Beloved Pack of Fools (Read Aloud for Full Effect)."

Billy tried to grab it. Darla hip-checked him into the cooler, which tipped and dumped twenty pounds of ice down the front of his overalls. He yelped and did the ice-down-the-pants dance, hopping from foot to foot while the family ignored him completely.

The porch went dead quiet except for Billy's teeth chattering from the ice melt. Then Zeke yelled, "BALLOON WAR!" and cannonballed into the remaining ice cooler for emphasis.

Maude folded the will slowly, a dangerous smile creeping across her face. "That conniving old buzzard. Even six feet under, he's turnin' us into a three-ring circus."

Down there, by lantern light, he'd written songs. The best—or worst, depending on your tolerance for puns—was "Cluckin' Heartbreak Blues," which he performed at every family gathering thereafter, usually after his fourth glass of scuppernong.

Maude could still hear it, word for miserable word:

(Verse 1)
I dressed up my hens in bow ties so fine,
Thought they'd tote them rings right down the line.
But them faithless fowl took one look at freedom's door,
Flapped off with my dreams and left me on the floor.
(Chorus)
Oh, cluckin' heartbreak, peck away at my pride,
Love flew the coop and left me dead inside.
I do'd and I don't'd, but mostly I cried,
Singin' these bunker blues till the day that I died.
Cluck-a-doo-doo, baby, what'd you do?
My chickens done left me—and I reckon you did too.

(Verse 2)
Smoke filled the barn like a bad divorce fog,
Couples swapped partners like a square-dance hog.

Daddy with shotgun, groom hittin' the gas,
I blessed that tin-can get away on my rhinestone ass.
(Bridge – slow and weepy)
Now I'm ten feet down with my beans and my tears,
Dreamin' of poultry and wasted years.
If love's just a barnyard scam, then I'm the biggest fool,
'Cause I traded my heart for a couple of tools.

(Final Chorus)
Oh, cluckin' heartbreak, peck away at my pride!
Love flew the coop and left me dead inside!
Cluck-a-doo-doo, baby, one last adieu—
My chickens done left me... hell, I reckon I'm through.

Back in the present, Billy had finally stopped shivering and was already sketching balloon designs on a napkin with a crayon Zeke handed him. Junior was pricing scrap silk on his phone. Darla looked like she was calculating how many therapy sessions this would take.

Maude tucked the will into her apron pocket and surveyed her soggy, toupee-askew, ice-traumatized family.

"Alright, you lunatics. If we're buildin' a balloon, we start tomorrow. But first, somebody fish Reverend Potts outta that swing and find his dignity. It's probably under the petunias with Zeke."

A hot gust of wind rattled the porch chimes. The armadillo, still upright, seemed to nod approvingly. Earl was definitely laughing somewhere. And the festival hadn't even hit lunchtime yet.

Chapter 4:

Junkyard Jamboree and the Great Tarp Tangle

The next morning broke over Weatherford like a dropped plate—loud, messy, and impossible to ignore. Roosters crowed off-key, the sun glared like it had a grudge, and Maude Hargrove was already on her third cup of coffee, barking orders from the porch like a drill sergeant in house slippers.

"Up and at 'em, you lazy heathens! We got a balloon to build, and I ain't losin' this farm to some fool who thinks 'junk' means the inside of Billy's brain!"

Billy, Darla, and Junior had been drafted into the Great Hot Air Balloon Project, whether they liked it or not. Zeke and the grandkids were "scouting crew." Reverend Potts had wisely stayed home to pray for everyone's souls—and probably to superglue his toupee back on.

First stop: Old Man Pritchard's Junkyard, ten miles down a dirt road so rutted it could rattle the teeth out of a mule. Pritchard—Big Hank's uncle and the same Hank who'd chased a groom with a shotgun back in '03—ran the place like a dragon hoarding rusty treasure. He charged admission just to walk the aisles, and if you tried to haggle, he'd sic his three-legged dog, Stumpy, on your ankles.

The Hargrove caravan rolled in just after nine: Maude's ancient Suburban pulling Junior's flatbed trailer, Billy riding shotgun with a notebook full of manic sketches, Darla in her sensible sedan bringing up the rear, and Zeke hanging out the window yelling "Balloon or bust!"

Pritchard met them at the gate, overalls stained with thirty years of grease, chewing tobacco like it owed him money.

"Maude Hargrove," he drawled, spitting a stream that landed perilously close to Billy's boot. "Heard y'all are tryin' to out-crazy Earl. That's a tall order."

Maude handed over a jar of her prize-winning chow-chow as a bribe or entry fee. "We need silk. Lots of it. Old parachutes, tents, wedding dresses—anything that'll hold hot air without catchin' fire too quick." Pritchard grinned, revealing a gold tooth shaped like Texas. "Aisle seven. But watch your step. Place is booby-trapped against thieves."

He wasn't kidding.

The hunt began innocently enough. Billy spotted a pile of vintage Army surplus parachutes and dove in headfirst like a gopher into fresh dirt. "Jackpot! Nylon's perfect—lightweight, strong, and government-approved!"

He yanked one free. It unfurled like a monster waking up, billowing out and snagging on a stack of rusted bedframes. The frames toppled in a domino wave, clanging like a xylophone from hell. One bedframe catapulted a hubcap that ricocheted off a washing machine and beaned Junior square in the forehead.

Junior dropped like a sack of feed, phone flying. Zeke caught it mid-air and kept recording. "Content gold!"

Darla rushed over. "You, okay?" Junior sat up, lump rising like bread dough. "Define okay."

Meanwhile, Maude had found a stack of old circus tents—faded red and white stripes, perfect for drama.

She tugged the corner of the top one. It didn't budge. She tugged harder. The entire stack shifted, then avalanched, burying her up to the waist in musty canvas. "Little help!" her muffled voice demanded.

Billy and Darla grabbed folds and pulled. The tent came free with a whoosh, launching Maude backward into a pile of discarded trampolines. She bounced once—high—flailing like a turtle on its back, landed on the edge of one, and shot forward again, straight into Pritchard's prize collection of porcelain garden gnomes.

Crash. Tinkle. Smash.
Twenty-seven gnomes became twenty-seven piles of pointy-hat confetti. Pritchard's face went the color of a ripe tomato.
"Those were vintage!" he roared.
Maude extricated herself, covered in canvas dust and gnome shards. "Send the bill to Earl's ghost."

The real chaos started when they found the motherlode: a shipping container full of discarded hot air balloon envelopes from a failed Tulsa festival in the '90s. Gorgeous colors—sunburst orange, electric blue, one with a giant smiling cowboy face.

Billy climbed the container like a monkey on moonshine, yelling, "I'll toss 'em down!" He grabbed the first envelope and gave it a mighty heave. It unfolded mid-air, inflating slightly from the breeze and turning into a 40-foot parachute of slippery nylon. It drifted down slowly—right over Darla, who was bending over to pick up a basket wicker.

The envelope settled over her like a giant jellyfish. She shrieked, stumbled blindly, arms pinwheeling, and crashed into Zeke, who crashed into Junior, who crashed into the trailer hitch.

Chain reaction: Junior's foot caught the trailer's emergency brake release. The flatbed—already half-loaded with scrap—rolled backward down the slight incline, gathering speed.

Pritchard himself dove out of the way just as the trailer smashed through the door, emerging out the back wall dragging the shack's entire front porch with it like a bad toupee.

Then the pièce de résistance: the giant cowboy-face envelope, still half-inflated from Billy's toss, caught a gust. It lifted off the ground, dragging its gondola basket—miraculously intact—behind it like a reluctant dog on a leash.

The basket snagged Billy's ankle as it passed. He yelped, lost his balance on the container roof, and got yanked off, sailing through the air dangling upside down, overalls flapping like surrender flags.

He flew twenty feet, arms windmilling, screaming "This is how I die!" before the envelope lost lift and deposited him gently—but face-first—into a pile of discarded feather mattresses.

Feathers exploded in a white mushroom cloud. When it settled, Billy emerged looking like a deranged chicken, coughing plumes of down.

Darla, still tangled in nylon, finally fought free just in time to see the damage: gnome graveyard, oil slick, demolished shack, and her brother wearing a feather boa he hadn't asked for.

Junior, lump and all, limped over with the phone. "We're at three hundred thousand views already. Hashtag HargroveChaos is trending in Oklahoma." Pritchard stood amid the wreckage, staring at the trailer protruding from his former office like a bad piercing.

Maude hauled herself up, oil-streaked and gnome-dusted, and brushed feathers off Billy's head. "Well," she said, surveying the carnage with grim satisfaction, "we got our silk. And a basket. And enough nylon to cover Texas."

She turned to Pritchard, who looked ready to commit homicide.

"Put it on Earl's tab," she said, slapping another jar of chow-chow into his hand. "He's good for it. Eventually."

As they loaded what they could salvage—under Pritchard's thunderous glare and Stumpy's enthusiastic ankle-nipping—the wind kicked up again. A single gnome hat, miraculously intact, tumbled across the yard and came to rest at Maude's feet. She picked it up, dusted it off, and stuck it on Billy's feathered head.

"There. Now you look like the grand marshal of crazy."

Billy grinned through the down, eyes already sparkling with the next terrible idea. Back at the farm, the real building was about to begin.

And God help Weatherford.

Chapter 5:

Festival Setup Shenanigans and the Propane Prophecy

By Thursday, the Pa's Folly Festival grounds—twenty acres of Hargrove pasture ringed by food trucks, carnival rides rented from a sketchy outfit in Tulsa, and enough portable toilets to service a small army—looked like a war zone designed by a committee of drunk toddlers.

Maude had declared an all-hands setup day. Booths needed raising, banners hanging, games rigging, and—most importantly—the balloon-building zone fencing off before Billy accidentally incinerated the petting zoo.

The day started promisingly. At 7 a.m., the family gathered around the kitchen table with coffee, biscuits, and Maude's battle plan scribbled on the back of an old seed catalog.

"Billy," Maude said, pointing with a gravy-smeared fork, "you and Junior handle the main stage and sound system. Darla, you're on games and booths with the grandkids. Zeke, you stay where I can see you. No fireworks till Saturday, hear?"

Zeke saluted with a biscuit in each hand. "Yes, ma'am. Scout's honor."

He'd been kicked out of Scouts at age nine for selling bootleg fireworks at camp.

Billy, still feathered from the junkyard and buzzing on four Red Bulls, was already sketching speaker placements. "I got this, Ma. I'm gonna rig Pa's old karaoke machine into the PA. Gonna blast 'Cluckin' Heartbreak Blues' on loop—give the place authentic atmosphere!"

Darla groaned. "Authentic migraine, you mean."

By eight, chaos was in full bloom.

First casualty: the banner.

Junior and Billy decided the festival's massive welcome banner—"PA'S FOLLY FESTIVAL: EARL WOULD BE PROUD (AND PROBABLY ON FIRE)"—needed to stretch across the entrance gate. They borrowed Pritchard's extension ladder (without asking) and hauled it out, along with a 40-foot vinyl banner rolled like a burrito.

Billy climbed the ladder first, banner rope clenched in teeth like a pirate. Junior fed from below. "Left a smidge!" Billy mumbled around nylon.
Junior tugged. The banner unrolled too fast, whipping like a sail in the breeze. It caught the wind, ballooned out, and yanked Billy clean off the ladder. He dangled ten feet up, legs bicycling air, while the banner flapped around him like a patriotic straitjacket.
Junior tried anchoring it, but the rope burned through his hands. He let go. The banner snapped taut, slingshotting Billy into the portable sign that read "FESTIVAL PARKING →". The sign toppled, domino-style, into the row of porta-potties lined up for delivery.

Three toilets tipped. One door swung open mid-fall, revealing a very surprised—and very occupied—delivery driver who'd been using the facilities for a "test sit." The man shrieked. Billy, still tangled, crash-landed on the grass with the banner draped over him like a failed magic trick. The driver scrambled out, pants half-mast, and sprinted toward his truck, dignity trailing behind like toilet paper on a shoe.

Zeke filmed the whole thing. "Five stars. Would recommend."

Next: the dunk tank. Darla and the older grandkids, Ruby and Tad, were setting up the classic festival dunk tank—proceeds going to the volunteer fire department, victim to be the sheriff on Saturday. The tank was ancient, painted fire-engine red, with a seat rigged to a target.

Ruby, ever the influencer, insisted on testing it for content. "I'll sit, Tad throws. It'll go viral."

Tad, bookish and uncoordinated, wound up like a major-league pitcher. His first throw missed by three feet, beaning a stack of folding chairs instead. The chairs scattered like bowling pins, one launching into the cotton-candy machine someone had just plugged in.

The machine whirred to life prematurely, spewing pink floss like a volcano. It coated Tad head to toe in sticky webs. Blinded, he staggered backward, tripped over a cooler, and fell butt-first into the dunk tank—seat and all.

The seat collapsed under his weight. The entire tank tipped forward, dumping 300 gallons of ice-cold water in a tidal wave that swept across the midway.

Darla, standing closest, got hit full force. The wave lifted her off her feet and deposited her ten yards away in the bounce house that hadn't been inflated yet. She landed in a heap of vinyl, flailing like a turtle until Ruby hauled her out—drenched, hair plastered, mascara running in black streaks.

Ruby, phone still recording, narrated breathlessly: "Family bonding, Oklahoma style. Ten out of ten."

Meanwhile, Billy had moved on to the propane heaters for the evening chili cook-off. He'd "improved" Earl's old design: twenty-pound tanks linked by garden hoses and duct tape, with a central ignition switch made from a barbecue lighter and pure optimism.

"Safety first!" he declared, then flipped the master switch to test.
Nothing happened.
He jiggled wires. Still nothing.

He smacked the manifold with a wrench—classic percussion maintenance.
A spark jumped. Every tank ignited at once with a deafening WHOOMPH, shooting blue flames three feet high. The sudden heat melted the duct tape seals. One hose popped loose, whipping like an

angry cobra, spraying propane and knocking over the row of chili cauldrons waiting to be filled.

She put two fingers in her mouth and whistled sharp enough to shatter glass. The hose chose that moment to run out of pressure and flop lifelessly at Billy's feet.

Silence fell, broken only by the distant wail of the delivery driver's truck peeling out of the parking lot.

Maude planted her hands on her hips. "Y'all got till sundown to fix this mess, or I'm sellin' the farm to the highest bidder and movin' to Branson."
Billy, singed eyebrows and all, grinned maniacally. "But Ma, we're makin' progress! This is just like Pa's setups—starts with disaster, ends with legend!"

Darla wrung out her shirt. "Legendary disaster, you mean."

Zeke popped up from behind the cauldron, grass-stained and triumphant, holding his phone aloft. "We just hit a million views. Hashtag FollySetupFail is number one trending!"

Maude looked heavenward. A single cloud drifted by, shaped suspiciously like Earl giving a thumb-up. Festival opened in forty-eight hours.
God help them all.

Chapter 6:

Balloon Assembly Blowups and the Great Envelope Entanglement

Friday dawned with the kind of Oklahoma heat that could melt asphalt and tempers in equal measure. The festival opened tomorrow, and the Hargrove balloon—still more concept than craft—needed to be assembled in the back pasture before sundown or the whole inheritance challenge was bust.

Maude had declared the pasture off-limits to festival traffic, roping it off with caution tape and a hand-painted sign: "BALLOON ZONE: TRESPASSERS WILL BE LAUNCHED." She'd also commandeered every fan, extension cord, and leaf blower on the property for the inflation test.

The family assembled at noon, looking like survivors of a minor war: Billy singed and feathered, Darla still faintly pink from cotton-candy residue, Junior sporting a goose-egg lump, and Zeke buzzing on funnel-cake sugar.

The "envelope"—a Frankenstein patchwork of junkyard nylon, circus tent scraps, and the giant cowboy-face panel—was spread across the grass like a dead rainbow. The wicker basket sat nearby, reinforced with duct tape and prayers. A rack of propane tanks and two industrial shop fans completed the setup.

Billy, in full manic inventor mode, clapped his hands like a hype man. "Operation Sky High Hargrove commences! Step one: cold inflate to check seams. Junior, fire up the fans!"

Junior plugged in the twin leaf blowers—borrowed from the church lawn crew—and aimed them into the envelope's open neck. The nylon billowed promisingly. For thirty glorious seconds, it looked like success.
Then the first mishap struck.

One blower's cord, frayed from years of abuse, sparked against the metal rack. The spark jumped to a loose flap of nylon that Billy had "sealed" with spray adhesive and glitter (for flair). The adhesive, apparently flammable, whooshed into a blue flame that raced along the seam like a fuse.
Billy dove for a fire extinguisher, yanked the pin, and blasted—directly into the blower intake. Foam exploded backward in a white blizzard, coating Junior head to toe and gumming up the blower blades. The

blower screamed, overheated, and shot out of Junior's hands like a rocket, ricocheting off the basket and embedding itself in the side of Maude's tool shed.

Junior, now a human snowman, slipped on the foam-slick grass and sat down hard on a propane regulator. The valve hissed open. Propane jetted out, turning the foam into a slippery, flammable bubble bath.

Darla grabbed a garden hose to douse the seam fire. She cranked the spigot full blast—forgetting Maude had hooked it to the pressure booster for the petting-zoo misting fans. The hose bucked like a bronco, whipping out of her grip and spraying a high-pressure jet that knocked Zeke clean off his feet and into the half-inflated envelope.

Zeke bounced inside the nylon like a human pinball, yelling "Wheeee!" until the envelope, now slippery with foam and water, collapsed around him in a giant, writhing blob.

Billy, trying to heroically stomp out the seam fire, slipped in the propane-foam slurry and belly-flopped onto the envelope. His weight trapped Zeke inside and pinned Darla's foot. Darla yanked free, lost balance, and toppled into the basket, which—thanks to uneven ground—rolled downhill toward the cattle pond.

The basket picked up speed, dragging the tangled envelope (with Billy and Zeke still inside) behind it like a monstrous nylon parachute. Junior, half-blind from foam in his eyes, chased after it, arms windmilling.

Maude watched the spectacle from the fence line, coffee mug frozen halfway to her lips.

The basket hit a bump, launched airborne for a heart-stopping second, then splashed into the pond with a magnificent cannonball splash. The envelope followed, billowing over the water like a deflating jellyfish.

Billy surfaced first, sputtering and covered in pond scum, still clutching the fire extinguisher like a teddy bear. Zeke popped up next, grinning ear to ear, algae draped over his head like a victory wreath. Darla, clinging to the basket rim, looked ready to commit fratricide.

Junior arrived at the pond's edge, slipped on mud, and executed a perfect face-plant into the cattails. For a moment, the only sounds were bullfrogs croaking and the hiss of escaping propane back at the assembly site.

Then Zeke yelled, "Again! Again!"

Maude finally moved. She marched down the hill, grabbed Billy by the ear (he was closest), and hauled him out like a misbehaving cat.

"Y'all have exactly one hour to drag that soggy mess outta my pond, dry it, patch it, and get it inflated proper," she barked. "Or I swear on Earl's rusty urn, I'll tie the lot of you inside it and light the burner myself."

Billy, dripping and sheepish, raised a hand. "But Ma, the seams held! Mostly! That's progress!"
Darla, wringing pond water from her hair, muttered, "Progress toward Darwin Awards."

Junior, spitting cattail fluff, checked his phone—miraculously dry—and whooped. "Two million views on the live stream. We're famous!"
Maude snatched the phone, ended the stream, and pointed at the pond.
"Fish it out. Patch it. Or sleep in it tonight. Your choice."

As the family waded in to retrieve the sodden envelope—slipping, splashing, and cursing the entire way—a hot breeze rustled the pasture grass.

Somewhere in the distance, a laugh that sounded suspiciously like Earl's echoed across the water.
The balloon wasn't flying yet.
But it was definitely making waves.

Chapter 7:

Gertie's Grand Entrance and the Tornado-Warning Tête-à-Tête

Saturday morning arrived like a hangover after a three-day bender: slow, mean, and full of regrets. The Pa's Folly Festival officially opened at ten sharp, but by nine-thirty the midway was already packed—folks lining up for funnel cakes, turkey legs, and the privilege of watching the Hargroves make fools of themselves in real time.

The balloon, miraculously, was almost ready. After Friday's pond fiasco, Maude had locked everyone in the barn until midnight with sewing machines, patch kits, and a single rule: no talking unless it was about stitches. The envelope now lay spread across the pasture again, patched in a dozen shades of duct tape and desperation, the giant cowboy face grinning crookedly at one end like it knew something nobody else did. The basket sat upright, burner rigged and tested (three times, with Maude holding the fire extinguisher personally).
That's when the pink Cadillac convertible rolled in.

The woman stepped out, all curves and confidence, and hollered in a voice that carried like a church bell: "Maude Hargrove, you old battle-ax! Get over here and hug my neck!"

Maude's coffee mug stopped halfway to her lips. The color drained from her face faster than milk from a kicked pail.

"Gertie Lou Maynard," she said, voice flat as a busted tire. "I thought you were still in Branson singin' backup for dead Elvis impersonators."

Gertie laughed—a big, brassy sound that turned heads all the way to the funnel-cake stands. "Honey, I upgraded. Now I'm in Vegas, singin' lead for live ones. But I heard my favorite family was puttin' on a show, and I just had to come see."

She strutted forward in rhinestone-studded cowboy boots, hips swaying like a metronome set to "trouble." Billy's jaw dropped. Junior's tip jar forgotten, he started filming. Ruby whispered, "Icon alert," and zoomed in.

Darla, who'd been restaking caution tape, froze. "Ma… isn't that the Gertie? The one from Pa's stories?"

Maude didn't answer. She just set her mug down very carefully, like it might explode.

Gertie reached the fence, leaned over it, and planted a lipstick-red kiss on Maude's cheek before Maude could dodge. "Look at you, still pretty as a speckled pup. And the farm—Lord, it's exactly the same. Even smells like Earl's bad decisions."

Maude wiped her cheek with the back of her hand. "What do you want, Gertie?"

"Can't a girl visit old friends?" Gertie batted fake lashes. Then her gaze drifted to the balloon, and her grin widened. "Though I gotta say, that hot air monstrosity looks familiar. Earl never did finish his, did he? Always said he'd take me up in one someday."

The air around the pasture went thick as sorghum syrup.

Billy found his voice first. "You knew Pa's balloon plans?"

Gertie turned to him, eyes twinkling. "Sugar, I knew a lot of Earl's plans. Some of 'em horizontal."

Darla made a choking sound. Junior whispered, "Plot twist."

Maude's voice cut through like a machete. "Gertie Lou, if you came here to stir ancient dirt, you could turn that pink monstrosity around and head back to Sin City."

Gertie held up both hands, palms out. "Now, now, no need for hostility. I came in peace—and with proof." She reached into the Cadillac's glove box and pulled out a manila envelope thick as a romance novel. "But maybe we should talk private-like. Family business."

Maude stared at the envelope like it was a rattlesnake wearing lipstick.

Before anyone could answer, the sky darkened. Not dramatically—just the sudden, sullen gray that Oklahoma natives know in their bones. The wind shifted, carrying the smell of rain and electricity. Sirens wailed in the distance: the county tornado warning.

Festivalgoers started scrambling. Food-truck awnings flapped. Someone yelled, "Bunker!"

Maude didn't hesitate. "Everybody to Earl's bunker! Move!"

The Hargroves had drilled this since childhood. They herded grandkids, grabbed essentials (Zeke snagged his phone, Ruby her ring light, Tad his notebook), and ran. Gertie, to her credit, didn't argue—she just grabbed her envelope and sprinted alongside Maude in those ridiculous boots.

Earl's bunker sat half-buried behind the barn: concrete hatch, reinforced door, built during one of his paranoid lows when he was convinced the government was coming for his moonshine recipe. Inside: cots, canned goods, a battery radio, and walls covered in Earl's manic scribbles—blueprints, song lyrics, and one memorable doodle of a squirrel in a straitjacket.

They piled in just as the rain hit—hard, sideways pellets that sounded like buckshot on the hatch. Maude slammed the door, spun the wheel, and flipped on the single bulb.

Eight people in a space meant for four. Wet, breathing hard, and—thanks to Gertie—loaded with more tension than a banjo string.
Billy broke the silence. "So… anybody bring cards?"
Zeke piped up, "Or snacks?"
Gertie settled onto a cot, crossing her legs like she owned the place. "I brought something better." She held up the envelope. "But it can wait till the twister passes. Or till Maude stops lookin' like she wants to taxidermy me next."

Maude leaned against the wall, arms folded. "Talk."
Gertie sighed theatrically. "Fine. Spoiler alert: I ain't just here for the festival." She opened the envelope

and pulled out a birth certificate, a stack of old photos, and a letter in Earl's handwriting.

She handed the birth certificate to Maude.
Name: Gertrude Earl Hargrove-Maynard.
Father: Earl Theodore Hargrove.
Mother: Gertie Lou Maynard.

The bunker went quieter than a church mouse with laryngitis.
Darla whispered, "No freaking way."
Billy's eyes went wide—the manic glitter replaced by pure shock. "Pa had a… secret daughter?"

Gertie smiled, softer now. "Born in '82. Maude, you were pregnant with Darla Sue at the time, and Earl was… well, Earl. High as a kite, convinced he was gonna be a country star. We had a fling. I left town before I started showin'. Raised her—me—on the road. But Earl sent money when he could. And letters."

She held up the photos: a younger Gertie holding a baby with Earl's unmistakable ears. Earl in his Elvis jumpsuit, grinning beside a toddler on a mechanical pony. Earl and teenage Gertie backstage somewhere, arms around each other.

Maude stared at the pictures for a long, terrible moment. Then she looked up at Gertie—not with anger, but something sadder.
"You're tellin' me I've got another stepchild I never knew about?"

Gertie nodded. "And accordin' to Oklahoma law, that makes me eligible for inheritance too. But I ain't here to take the farm, Maude. I came because… well, because Earl's dying words to me on the phone were 'Tell Maude I'm sorry, and tell the kids to finish the damn balloon.'"
Thunder boomed overhead. The radio crackled with the weather alert: tornado on the ground five miles west, moving east.
Junior finally spoke. "So… Aunt Gertie?"

Gertie grinned. "In the flesh, nephew."

Zeke, ever practical, asked, "Does this mean more presents at Christmas?"

Outside, the wind howled like a banshee with a grudge. Inside, the family sat stunned, the weight of thirty-eight years of secrets pressing down harder than any storm.

Maude finally exhaled a long, shaky breath. She reached over and patted Gertie's knee, awkward but genuine.

"Well," she said, voice steady again, "if you're Earl's, you're stuck with us. But you try singin' karaoke in my house, and we'll have words."

Gertie laughed through sudden tears. "Deal."

The radio crackled again: tornado veering north, missing Weatherford.

The storm wasn't over.

But in the bunker, something new had just begun.

Chapter 8:

Reverend Potts's Pasture Therapy and the Pie-Poisoning Plot

Sunday morning after the tornado scare dawned clear and mercilessly hot, the kind of heat that made the air shimmer like a bad mirage and turned every breath into soup. The festival was in full swing—crowds thicker than flies on a pie cooling rack, kids screaming on the Zipper ride, and the smell of fried onions and desperation thick in the air.

But in the Hargrove back pasture, under a rented white canopy that flapped like surrender flags, the family was engaged in something far more dangerous than carnival rides: mandatory group therapy.

Reverend Potts, still sporting a faint toupee tan line and clutching his Bible like a riot shield, had declared an "emergency pastoral intervention" after Gertie's bombshell. He'd shown up at dawn with a folding table, eight mismatched lawn chairs, a pitcher of iced tea (spiked with his own "medicinal" peach schnapps), and the serene confidence of a man who'd never actually studied counseling.

Maude had agreed only because the balloon needed drying time after yesterday's storm rinse, and because Potts threatened to preach a sermon titled "The Wages of Secret Sin" if they refused.

So there they sat in a lopsided circle: Maude ramrod straight in the middle, Darla with arms crossed so tight her knuckles went white, Billy fidgeting like a kid on Red Bull (which he was), Junior filming discreetly from behind a hay bale, Gertie lounging like a Vegas showgirl on break, and the grandkids banished to the fence line with strict orders to "observe silently or face dish duty till Christmas."

Reverend Potts cleared his throat, adjusted his toupee (still slightly askew), and began.

"Brothers and sisters—well, mostly sisters plus Billy—let us open with prayer." He bowed his head. "Lord, grant us the serenity to accept the Hargroves we cannot change, the courage to survive the ones we can, and the wisdom to know when to duck. Amen."

Zeke, from the fence, whispered loudly, "Amen, and pass the popcorn."
Potts ignored him. "Today's session is about forgiveness. And communication. And—" he glanced at Gertie "—acknowledging certain... historical overlaps."

Gertie raised a manicured hand. "You mean my daddy sleepin' with your parishioner while she was pregnant with number two? That overlap?"

Darla made a strangled noise. Billy's eyes went wide and manic. Maude stared straight ahead like she was calculating how many taxidermy pins it would take to mount a reverend.

Potts plowed on, sweating through his seersucker. "Let's use the talking stick method." He held up a decorative corncob pipe Earl had once carved during a low. "Whoever holds the pipe speaks without interruption."
He handed it to Maude first.

Maude took it, turned it over once, then snapped it in half.
"Talking stick's broken," she said. "My turn anyway. Gertie, I ain't mad you exist. I'm mad Earl kept you secret like a bad report card. But you're here now, and you're blood, so you get a chair at the table. Just don't expect me to call you 'daughter' till you've survived at least one Thanksgiving."

Gertie's eyes misted. "Fair enough, Mama Maude."
Maude winced. "Let's stick with Maude."
The pipe—well, the two halves—passed to Darla.

Darla gripped her half like a dagger. "I spent years thinking Pa was just a chaotic flake who loved Ma more than anything. Finding out he had a whole secret kid feels like… like someone told me Santa was real and also a deadbeat." She glared at Gertie. "No offense."

Gertie shrugged. "None taken. I grew up knowing exactly who Daddy was—flaws, Elvis jumpsuit, and all."

Billy grabbed the other half of the pipe before it reached him officially. "This is great! More family means more crew for the balloon! Gertie, you any good with a torch? I'm thinkin' we add pyrotechnics for the launch—roman candles around the basket rim, spell out 'EARL LIVES' in sparks!"

Potts tried to intervene. "Billy, focus on feelings, not flammables."

Billy waved him off. "My feelings are ignited, Rev! This inheritance challenge just got epic!" Junior, still filming, leaned in. "Also, views are through the roof. #HargroveFamilyTherapy is trending."

Potts pinched the bridge of his nose. "Lord, give me strength."

That's when the pie arrived.

A shadow fell over the circle. Everyone looked up to see Clyde McAllister—head of the rival McAllister clan, owners of the biggest spread in three counties and perpetual Hargrove nemeses—standing at the edge of the canopy holding a lattice-top cherry pie the size of a tractor tire.

Clyde was tall, smug, and wore a bolo tie with a silver steer head the size of a dinner plate. Behind him lurked his twin sons, Bubba and Buddy, both built like refrigerators with legs.

"Afternoon, y'all," Clyde drawled, smile sharp as barbed wire. "Heard you were havin' a family meetin'. Thought I'd bring dessert—my wife's blue-ribbon cherry. Consider it a peace offerin'."

Maude eyed the pie as if it might be rigged with dynamite. "Clyde McAllister, the last time you brought food to this farm, my hogs got drunk on fermented persimmons and rooted up your north fence."

Clyde chuckled. "Ancient history. Besides, festival spirit and all." He set the pie on the table right in front of Gertie. "Help yourselves."

Something about the way he lingered, the way Bubba and Buddy smirked, set every Hargrove alarm bell ringing.

Darla leaned over and sniffed discreetly. "Smells… off. Like cherry and… bleach?"

Gertie, never one to refuse free dessert, had already cut a slice. She raised it to her lips.

Maude's hand shot out like a striking cobra and slapped the fork away. The slice flew, landing face-down in Reverend Potts's lap. Cherries exploded across his white pants like a crime scene.

"Hey!" Potts yelped, jumping up. Pie slid down his legs in red globs.

Billy grabbed the pie tin, sniffed, then dipped a finger and tasted the crust. His face went green. "Laxatives. Industrial strength. This thing's laced enough to evacuate Tulsa."

Clyde's smile faltered for half a second before snapping back. "Now, why would I do a thing like that?"

Maude stood slowly, all five-foot-four of her radiating wrath. "Because you heard about Earl's will. You want this farm when we lose the challenge. Figured if we're all huggin' the toilet tomorrow, we can't launch the balloon."
The McAllisters backed up a step.

Junior, still filming, narrated quietly: "And here comes the payback."
Zeke, from the fence, suddenly yelled, "Incoming!" and lobbed something overhand.

It was a water balloon—filled not with water, but with the leftover pond scum from yesterday's disaster. It arced perfectly and splattered across Clyde's bolo tie, coating the silver steer in green slime. Ruby followed with a second—this one packed with leftover cotton-candy fluff. It burst on Bubba's head, turning his hair into a sticky pink afro.

Tad, quiet Tad, surprised everyone by hurling a third—filled with Maude's homemade chow-chow. It exploded on Buddy's boots in a vinegar tsunami. The McAllisters retreated, slipping and cursing, as the Hargrove grandkids pelted them with festival ammunition like a well-trained militia.

Reverend Potts, still pie-stained, tried to restore order. "Violence is not the answer!"

Maude handed him a spare chow-chow balloon. "Then hold this, Rev."

Potts looked at it, looked at the fleeing McAllisters, and—after a moment's hesitation—lobbed it with surprising accuracy. It nailed Clyde square between the shoulder blades. Clyde roared and ran faster.

When the last McAllister vanished around the petting zoo, the therapy circle erupted—not in tears, but in laughter. Belly-holding, tear-streaming laughter.

Gertie wiped her eyes. "Daddy would've loved this."
Darla, still giggling, admitted, "Okay, that felt good."
Billy pumped a fist. "Family united! Now let's weaponize the balloon!"
Maude allowed herself a small, fierce smile. "First, we test that envelope for real. Then we deal with the McAllisters. Nobody poisons my people and walks away."

Reverend Potts looked down at his ruined pants, then at the broken corncob pipe, and finally at the pie tin now being used as a frisbee by Zeke.
"Maybe," he said faintly, "next session we try trust falls."

From somewhere in the pasture, a gust of wind rattled the balloon envelope, making the giant cowboy face seem to wink.

The therapy had worked—Hargrove style.

And the real mayhem was just warming up.

Chapter 9:

Gertie's Ghost Stories and the Balloon Basket Blunder

The therapy canopy had barely been folded away before Billy was back at it, dragging the family into the balloon-building frenzy like a tornado sucking up trailer parks. The pasture hummed with activity—propane tanks hissing test bursts, nylon seams getting triple-stitched, and the giant cowboy-face envelope billowing in the hot afternoon breeze like it was trying to wink at passersby. Festival crowds milled nearby, snapping photos and placing bets on whether the Hargroves would achieve liftoff or just a spectacular fireball.

Gertie, now officially drafted into the crew, rolled up her leopard-print sleeves and dove in with Vegas flair. "Alright, kinfolk, hand me that soldering iron. I once rigged a stage light show for a Celine Dion tribute that could blind a bald eagle. This basket needs some sparkle."

Billy eyed her warily but passed the tool. "Just don't turn it into a disco ball. We need structural integrity, not strobe lights."

Darla snorted, wrestling a roll of duct tape. "Integrity? From a family that once built a rollercoaster out of tractor parts. Good luck."

As they worked—Billy over-engineering the burner manifold with enough valves to rival a pipe organ, Junior pawning Maude's antique pie safe for extra propane fittings—conversation turned to Gertie. The therapy session had cracked the door on her past, but like a stubborn storm cellar hatch, it needed prying open.

Maude, patching a seam with needle and fishing line, finally broke the ice. "So, Gertie Lou, you said Earl sent letters. What'd that old fool write about? His squirrel wars or his bunker ballads?"

Gertie laughed, soldering a reinforcement strut onto the wicker basket. Sparks flew like fireflies on a meth binge. "Oh, a bit of both. But mostly stories. Tall tales mixed with Okie lore he picked up from his grandpappy. You know, the kind that make you wonder if it's moonshine or magic talkin'."

Zeke, perched on a hay bale with a welding mask flipped up like a knight's visor, leaned in. "Like what? Ghosts? Bigfoot? The Oklahoma Octopus?"

Gertie's eyes twinkled. "Better. Let me tell y'all about the first time Earl took me huntin' for the Spiro Mounds spirits. I was eight, summer of '90, and he'd just swung into one of his highs after a low that had him hidin' in a Tulsa motel for a week."

The pasture faded as Gertie's voice wove the flashback, the family pausing their work to listen, tools idle in hands sticky with glue and grease.

It was dusk on the Arkansas Riverbanks, near the ancient Spiro Mounds—those old Mississippian ruins where Cherokee and Choctaw folks say the ancestors whisper secrets if you listen carefully. Earl had bundled little Gertie into his rusted Chevy, promising "an adventure bigger than Paul Bunyan's britches." He was as manic as a jackrabbit on jolt cola, eyes shining beneath his battered cowboy hat, while telling her tales of the mounds' guardians: shape-shifting deer women who lure fools into the mist, or the Little People—mischievous spirits no taller than a knee, who steal your socks or grant wishes if you leave 'em cornbread.

"Now, darlin'," Earl said, handing her a tiny lantern carved from a gourd (his own invention, complete with a firefly bulb that flickered erratically), "the Little People don't take kindly to greed. But if we offer 'em somethin' pure—like this here acorn necklace I whittled—they might show us buried treasure. Gold from the old chiefs, or maybe just wisdom. Either way, jackpot!"

They crept through the tall grass, the river murmuring like it was gossiping with the wind. Gertie clutched the necklace, half-scared, half-thrilled. Earl spun yarns: how the deer women danced under full moons, turning men to stone if they stared too long, or how the mounds held portals to the underworld, guarded by horned serpents that could summon storms.

Suddenly, a rustle in the bushes. Earl froze, whispering, "That's them! The Little People!" He yanked Gertie down, and they peeked through the reeds. Out popped not spirits, but a family of raccoons—bandit-masked and bold—raiding a picnic leftover from tourists.

Earl whooped with laughter, scaring the critters off. "See? Folklore's just life with extra spice! But mark my words, girl, Oklahoma's full of magic. You just gotta squint to see it."

They didn't find treasure that night, but Earl pocketed a shiny river stone, swearing it was enchanted. Gertie wore the acorn necklace for years, convinced it brought luck—until it broke during her first Vegas audition, right before she landed the gig.

Back in the present, Gertie finished soldering and held up the strut. "That stone? Still on my keychain. And the stories? Kept me company on the road when Earl's letters stopped comin' regular."

Billy, inspired, grabbed a spare wicker strand and started weaving it into a crude horned serpent shape around the basket's rim. "We should add folklore flair! Make the balloon a flyin' tribute to the old spirits. Imagine: launch it with a chant to ward off tornadoes!"

Darla rolled her eyes but smiled despite herself. "Because nothing says 'safe ascent' like invoking mythical snakes."

Junior, ever the opportunist, snapped photos. "This'll sell tickets. #OkieFolkloreBalloon trending already."

Maude nodded slowly, her needle pausing. "Earl did love those tales. Said his bipolar swings were like the weather here—wild as a deer woman's dance. Highs like summer storms, lows like dust bowl droughts." Gertie's story sparked another flashback, this one from Maude's lips as they hoisted the envelope for a test inflation.

It was '85, Earl deep in a manic phase, convinced the family farm was haunted by the ghost of Belle Starr—the infamous outlaw queen who roamed Indian Territory robbin' stagecoaches and breakin' hearts. "She's buried secrets here," he'd declared one midnight, dragging Maude and a toddler Billy out with shovels and a map he'd "divined" from chicken bones.

Under a blood moon, they dug holes across the pasture, Earl spinning yarns of Belle's spectral horse thundering through the night, or her phantom laughter echoing in the wind. "Folks say she hides gold in places like this—cursed treasure that brings fortune or folly!"

The digging yielded nothing but arrowheads and a rusted spur—probably from some long-gone cowboy—but Earl swore it was Belle's, enchanted to protect against bad luck. He turned it into a keychain for Maude, who wore it grudgingly until it snagged her apron one too many times.

Come morning, the low hit. Earl retreated to the bunker, but not before whispering to Maude, "The real treasure's the stories, darlin'. Keeps the ghosts friendly."

Maude finished her tale just as they fired up the fans for the cold inflatable. The envelope rose slowly, majestically—until a seam Billy had "reinforced" with his serpent weave popped under pressure.

Nylon ripped with a sound like thunder. The envelope deflated in a chaotic whoosh, tangling around the basket and yanking it sideways. Billy dove to save it, tripped over a propane line, and face-planted into the wicker. The basket tipped, rolling like a tumbleweed and taking Gertie with it—she'd been inside testing the floor.

They tumbled twenty feet, a whirlwind of limbs and laughter, landing in a heap amid the petting zoo fence. Goats bleated in alarm, one nibbling Gertie's hair like it was folklore fodder.

Darla hauled them up, dusting off straw. "See? Invoking spirits just invites disaster." Gertie grinned, untangling a serpent strand from her boot. "Or adventure. Just like Daddy said."

Maude surveyed the mess, but her eyes held a spark. "Patch it again. And Gertie—tell us another one while we work. Might keep the Little People from trippin' us up."

As the family regrouped, a distant rumble echoed—not thunder, but the McAllisters' tractor revving ominously from their adjacent field. Sabotage was brewing. But with Gertie's stories flowing like river mist, the Hargroves felt a touch of that old Okie magic—wild, whimsical, and just a bit cursed.

Chapter 10:

The Great Balloon Burner Blowout and the Night the Deer Woman Danced

Monday of festival week hit like a cast-iron skillet to the forehead—humid, heavy, and promising pain. The Pa's Folly grounds were packed tighter than a tick on a hound, with lines for the funnel-cake trailer snaking clear to the porta-potties. Ruby's TikToks had gone supernova; half the state seemed to have shown up to watch the Hargroves either soar triumphantly or crash spectacularly.

In the back pasture, the balloon envelope lay spread like a patchwork quilt sewn by a committee of drunk quilting bees. Patches overlapped patches, duct tape crisscrossed like silver veins, and Billy's woven horned-serpent motif now coiled around the lower third in lopsided glory. The basket—reinforced, re-woven, and now sporting Gertie's rhinestone embellishments—sat ready for the burner assembly.

Billy, three days deep into a high that had him vibrating like a tuning fork, declared it "hot inflation day."
"Today we breathe fire into her lungs!" he announced, arms wide like a preacher at revival. "We'll tether her, test lift, and by Saturday she'll carry us all to glory!"

Maude eyed the rack of propane tanks warily. "Or to the burn unit. You triple-checked those lines?"

Billy waved a hand. "Quadruple. Plus, I added a failsafe—Pa's old pressure-release valve from the wedding-chapel fogger. Genius recycling!"

Darla muttered, "That's not recycling, that's Russian roulette with plumbing."

Gertie, ever the showwoman, had brought her portable karaoke machine and was warming up the crowd with a twangy cover of "Jolene" while helping Junior rig tether ropes to fence posts. Zeke darted between legs handing out "Official Hargrove Balloon Crew" stickers he'd printed on Maude's ancient label maker.

Work began at noon. Fans cold-inflated the envelope until it rose like a lazy rainbow over the pasture. Then came the moment of truth: lighting the burner.

Billy climbed into the basket with the reverence of a knight mounting his steed. He cracked the propane

valves, struck the pilot lighter, and—whoosh—blue flame roared to life, steady and strong.
For ten beautiful seconds, everything worked.

The envelope filled with hot air, lifting gently against the tethers. The cowboy face grinned down at them. Festivalgoers cheered from the fence line. Ruby's livestream chat exploded with rocket emojis.
Then the failsafe failed.

The old wedding-chapel valve—corroded from years of incense and neglect—stuck open. Pressure spiked. One hose whipped loose, spraying liquid propane like a garden sprinkler from hell.

Billy yelped and tried to throttle down, but the flame flared higher, licking the envelope's lower edge. A patch of circus-tent nylon—more flammable than anyone remembered—caught with a soft puff, then a louder whoosh.
Fire raced up the serpent weave like it was following a trail of gunpowder.

"Cut the fuel!" Maude roared.

Darla grabbed the main shutoff. Gertie yanked a tether rope. Junior dove for the fire extinguisher—only to discover Zeke had filled it with silly string "for pranks."

Flames climbed six feet, then ten. The envelope billowed wildly, tethers straining. One fence post snapped with a crack like gunfire. The basket lurched sideways, dragging across the grass and scattering goats like bowling pins.

Billy, still inside, clung to the rim shouting instructions nobody could hear over the roar. "Counterweight! Lean left! Embrace the chaos!"

Maude snatched the garden hose—pressure-boosted again—and blasted the flames. Water hit hot nylon and turned to steam, creating a swirling fog that made everything look like a low-budget horror movie.

In the midst of the steam and sparks, Gertie started laughing—big, uncontrollable Vegas-stage laughter. "Lord, it's just like the night Daddy swore he saw the Deer Woman!"

The family, soaked and singed, paused long enough for her to spin another flashback while they wrestled the burner offline.

Summer of '93. Earl, manic and convinced the farm was blessed by ancient spirits, had dragged teenage Gertie out at midnight during a full moon. He carried a mason jar of scuppernong wine "for offerings" and a boom box playing Patsy Cline.

"The Deer Woman's real, baby girl," he'd whispered as they crept through the tall grass near the pond. "Part beautiful maiden, part white-tailed doe. She dances for the worthy, leads the unworthy to their doom. If we're respectful, she'll bless the farm forever."

They left cornbread and a shiny quarter on a stump, then hid behind a hay bale. Hours passed. Crickets chirped. Mosquitoes feasted.

Then—movement. A graceful shape glided from the treeline: long hair flowing, legs flashing pale in the moonlight. It danced, spinning and leaping with impossible grace.
Earl gripped Gertie's arm, eyes wide. "There she is…"

The figure drew closer. Moonlight revealed antlers—no, a hat with feathers—and hooves that were actually muddy cowboy boots. It was Maude, in her nightgown, sneaking out to check on a colicky cow and doing a little tipsy twirl because the moon was pretty.

Earl and Gertie burst out laughing so hard they scared the real deer grazing nearby. Maude spotted them, marched over, and confiscated the wine. But she left the cornbread on the stump. "If the Deer Woman's real," she'd told them, "She's got better things to do than watch you two fools."

Back in the smoky pasture, the fire finally sputtered out—more from lack of fuel than heroism. The envelope sagged, blackened in patches but mostly intact. The basket listed sideways like a drunken sailor.
Billy climbed out, hair singed into an accidental mullet, face smeared with soot but grinning like a possum in a persimmon tree.

"We're alive! And she lifted! That counts as progress!"

Darla, dripping hose water, looked ready to strangle him. "Progress? We almost recreated the Hindenburg in 4K!"

Maude surveyed the damage, then the crowd was still filming from the fence. "Patch it. Again. But this time, no recycled parts older than Zeke."

Gertie wiped tears of laughter from her eyes. "Daddy always said the Deer Woman tests your mettle. Looks like we passed—barely."

Junior checked his phone. "Five million views. We're trending above Taylor Swift."

Zeke held up the empty silly-string extinguisher. "I can refill it with actual foam this time?"

Maude fixed him with a stare. "You refill it with holy water and an apology, young man."

As the family dragged out patch kits and fresh nylon—under a sky turning bruise-purple with evening storms—a lone white-tailed doe appeared at the treeline. It watched them for a long moment, ears flicking, then turned and vanished into the woods with a graceful bound.

Ruby zoomed in. "Was that…?" Darla snorted. "Probably just curious about the idiots setting their art project on fire."
But Gertie smiled softly. "Or maybe dancin' approval."
Billy, already sketching Version 9.0 of the burner, shouted, "Next try tomorrow! We're gettin' closer!"

Maude looked at the blackened envelope, the singed grass, and her soot-streaked family.
"Closer to what, exactly?" she muttered. "Glory or the ER?"

From the festival midway, faint music drifted back—someone playing "Cluckin' Heartbreak Blues" on the karaoke stage.

Earl was definitely watching.

And the balloon still wasn't ready.

Chapter 11:

Moonshine Karaoke and the Campfire Confessions

Tuesday night settled over the Hargrove farm like a warm, sticky blanket. The festival midway had shut down at ten—rides powered off, food trucks idling, the last funnel-cake sugar rush wearing off the kids. But in the back pasture, under a sky full of stars sharp enough to cut tin, the family gathered around a campfire built in an old wash-tub rim.

The balloon envelope lay folded nearby like a sleeping dragon, its blackened patches hidden in the dark. Tomorrow they'd patch and test again, but tonight Maude had declared a moratorium on work. "Y'all need food, rest, and somethin' stronger than sweet tea if we're gonna survive the week."

Junior had hauled out folding chairs, a cooler of beer, and—after a meaningful glare from Maude—only one mason jar of what he swore was "just peach preserves." Gertie plugged her karaoke machine into the generator, volume low enough not to wake the neighbors (or summon the sheriff). Zeke roasted marshmallows with the intensity of a bomb tech. Ruby and Tad shared one lawn chair, scrolling through the day's viral clips. Even Reverend Potts had wandered over, Bible tucked under his arm like he wasn't sure whether to preach or partake.

Billy, coming down from his manic peak and sliding toward the inevitable crash, sat quiet for once, staring into the flames. Darla nursed a beer, unusually relaxed. Maude presided from her rocker, passing out paper plates of brisket and beans like a queen doling out favors.

Gertie broke the comfortable silence first. "Daddy always said a campfire's where the real stories come out. Not the tall tales—the ones that hurt a little."

She queued up the karaoke machine. The tinny intro to "Cluckin' Heartbreak Blues" crackled through the speaker.
The family groaned in unison.
"No," Darla said. "Absolutely not."
"Yes," Maude countered, voice soft but firm. "Earl wrote it in the bunker after the chapel fiasco. Said it was the only honest thing he ever made. We're singin' it tonight. All of us."

Junior hit play before anyone could protest.
One by one, they took the mic—reluctant, off-key, but earnest.
Billy went first, voice cracking on the chorus: "Cluck-a-doo-doo, baby, what'd you do?" His eyes were red-

rimmed; the high was ebbing, leaving the familiar gray fog creeping in.

Darla followed, surprising everyone with a clear alto on the second verse. She changed "chickens" to "dreams" without thinking, and nobody corrected her. Junior hammed it up, adding chicken-cluck sound effects that made Zeke howl with laughter.

Gertie took the bridge, slow and weepy, Vegas polish giving way to raw Oklahoma gravel. She sang it like she'd lived every word of lost love and barnyard betrayal.

When Maude's turn came, she didn't stand. Just took the mic and sang from her chair, eyes on the fire. "Now I'm ten feet down with my beans and my tears…"
Her voice trembled only once—on the line about trading her heart for a couple of tools. The crack in it silenced even the crickets.

When the final chorus rolled around, they all joined in, a ragged, off-key family choir under the stars. Zeke provided percussion by banging a stick on the cooler. Reverend Potts, after a long pull from the "preserves" jar, added a surprisingly decent baritone harmony.

The song ended. For a long moment, nobody spoke. Then Darla said quietly, "I didn't know the lows were that bad for him."

Maude passed the jar to Gertie. "He hid 'em best he could. The highs were fireworks—everybody saw those. The lows… he carried alone, mostly. Thought admitting it made him less of a man."

Billy stared at his boots. "I get the highs. The ideas that feel like God himself whispered 'em. But the crash afterward… like the world goes mute."

Gertie nodded. "He wrote me once, said it was like chasin' a tornado—you ride the rush, then it drops you in a ditch wonderin' how you got there."

Reverend Potts cleared his throat. "Scripture calls it the thorn in the flesh. Paul begged God to take his away three times. God said, 'My grace is sufficient.' Maybe Earl's thorn was his wiring. But look what grew around it—y'all. This circus of love."

Zeke, sticky with marshmallow, piped up. "So, Pa's ghost ain't mad, right? He's just… watchin' us finish his balloon?"

Maude ruffled his hair. "If he's watchin', he's laughin'. And probably takin' bets on whether we blow ourselves up."

That earned chuckles. The tension eased.

Junior refilled cups. "Speakin' of blowin' up—anybody notice the McAllisters sneakin' around the fence line earlier? Looked like they were measurin' somethin'."

Darla frowned. "Probably plannin' more sabotage. That pie wasn't their finale."

Billy perked up slightly. "Let 'em try. We've got Okie magic on our side now." He nodded toward the folded envelope. "Deer Woman approved."

Gertie smiled. "And don't forget the Little People. I left cornbread on the stump again this afternoon. Just in case."

Tad, quiet until now, closed his notebook. "I've been writin' it all down. The stories, the songs, the disasters. If we survive this week, it's gonna be a book." Ruby elbowed him. "And I've got the footage. We split the profits?"
"Deal."

Maude raised her cup. "To Earl. To thorns and fireworks. To finishin' what he started—together." They clinked plastic cups and mason jars. The fire popped, sending sparks skyward like tiny hot-air balloons.
Somewhere in the dark beyond the firelight, a branch cracked. Everyone froze.

Zeke whispered, "Ghost?"
Junior shone his phone flashlight. Nothing but shadows and the glint of the balloon's cowboy face.

Darla laughed nervously. "Probably just a raccoon. Or the McAllisters."

Maude settled back in her rocker. "Either way, let 'em come. We've got a song in us now."

The karaoke machine, on its own or maybe nudged by an unseen hand, started the next track: Earl's favorite—Patsy Cline's "Crazy."

Gertie took the mic without hesitation and began to sing.

One by one, the others joined in.

The campfire burned lower. The stars wheeled overhead. And for the first time all week, the Hargroves felt less like a family cursed by madness and more like one held together by it.

Saturday's launch was four days away.

Whatever came next—McAllister sabotage, balloon triumph, or total folly—they'd face it singing.

Chapter 12:

The McAllister Midnight Raid and the Little People's Revenge

Wednesday crept in on little cat feet—quiet, sneaky, and ready to pounce. The festival hummed along like a well-oiled tractor: crowds thicker than ever, Ruby's follower count ticking past a million, and Junior's tip jar overflowing with bills from folks betting on launch-day disaster. But behind the midway glitter, tension coiled tighter than baling wire.

The Hargroves had patched the balloon once again. The envelope now resembled a quilt stitched by a committee of chain-smoking grandmas—functional, ugly, and strangely proud of it. Billy's latest burner redesign (Version 12: "The Phoenix") sat tested and tethered, flames steady in short bursts. One more full inflation tomorrow, then Friday for final tweaks. Saturday—launch or bust.

Maude had posted "guards" on rotating shifts: Darla with a thermos of coffee and a shotgun loaded with rock salt, Gertie with her karaoke machine rigged to blast show tunes at intruders, and Zeke with a slingshot and a pocket full of acorns "for the Little People."

At 2:17 a.m., the intruders came anyway.

Darla dozed in a lawn chair by the pasture gate, shotgun across her lap, when she heard the faint rumble of a side-by-side ATV. Headlights off, engine muffled—classic McAllister stealth. She snapped awake as three figures in black hoodies slipped through the fence: Clyde's twins, Bubba and Buddy, plus their cousin Duane (known county-wide for two things: bench-pressing refrigerators and having the IQ of a fence post).

They carried bolt cutters, a gallon jug of what smelled like kerosene, and smug expressions.

Darla chambered a round—loud enough to echo like judgment day.
The trio froze.

"Evenin', boys," Darla drawled. "Y'all lost? Burnin' Man's in Nevada."

Bubba recovered first, flashing a grin missing one front tooth. "Just takin' a stroll, Darla Sue. No harm."
Buddy hefted the jug. "Checkin' for fire hazards. Safety first."
Duane, not the sharpest, added helpfully, "We're gonna light your balloon up like the Fourth."

Darla sighed. "Duane, honey, that's confessin'. Makes the rock salt hurt less on my conscience."
She raised the shotgun.

The McAllister boys bolted—straight into the pasture, where Zeke had spent the evening "protecting" the balloon with his own special defenses.

First trap: fishing line strung knee-high across the grass, tied to cowbells Junior swiped from the petting zoo. Bubba hit it full tilt, legs tangling like a calf in barbed wire. He went down hard, bells clanging loud enough to wake half of Weatherford.

Second trap: the cornbread Zeke had left on stumps "for the Little People," now strategically placed in front of shallow holes dug that afternoon. Buddy stepped squarely on a crumbling piece, foot sinking into a hole lined with Maude's leftover chow-chow brine. He yelped as vinegar soaked his boot and slipped backward, jug flying.

The kerosene splashed across Duane's overalls instead of the balloon. Duane, panicking, dropped his lighter. It sparked.
Whoosh.

Blue flame raced up Duane's leg like gossip in a beauty parlor. He screamed—a high, undignified sound—and ran in circles, a human Roman candle.

Gertie's motion-sensor karaoke machine kicked on at the noise, blasting "Ring of Fire" at full volume. Johnny Cash's voice boomed across the pasture: "I fell into a burnin' ring of fire…"

Lights flicked on in the farmhouse. Maude appeared in her housecoat and mud boots, carrying the garden hose like a flamethrower in reverse. Billy, half-dressed and wild-eyed from a late-night idea spree, followed with the real fire extinguisher (refilled with actual foam this time).

They found chaos: Bubba tangled in fishing line, cursing and ringing bells; Buddy stuck in a chow-chow pit, boot smoking faintly; Duane rolling on the ground while Darla hosed him down, steam rising like morning fog.

Maude shut off the hose and surveyed the damage—none to the balloon, all to McAllister pride.

"Y'all got ten seconds to vacate my property before I switch from water to buckshot," she said calmly.

The twins hauled Duane up—pants charred, dignity incinerated—and limped toward the fence. Duane whimpered with every step.

As they retreated, Zeke popped up from behind a hay bale, slingshot in hand, grinning like a possum.

"The Little People helped!" he announced proudly. "I left 'em extra cornbread!"

Gertie, who'd arrived mid-hose-down, laughed until she wheezed. "Boy, if that ain't folklore comin' alive. Mischievous spirits, my foot—Earl's grandkid is the real trickster."

Billy stared at the untouched balloon, then at the retreating McAllisters, then at Zeke's traps. For once, he was speechless.

Darla lowered the shotgun, shaking her head. "We didn't even need the rock salt."

Maude coiled the hose. "Clean this mess before dawn. And Zeke—good job, baby. But next time, warn us so we don't shoot you by mistake."

Zeke saluted. "Yes, ma'am. Should I leave more cornbread tonight?"

Maude considered. "Double portion. Whoever's helpin' us earned it."

By sunrise, the pasture was pristine again—traps reset, kerosene mopped, bells re-hung. The balloon stood tethered and proud, cowboy face seeming to smirk at the fence line where faint ATV tracks led away.

Word of the midnight raid spread faster than head lice in kindergarten. By noon, festival attendance doubled. Folks came to see the balloon that survived arson, the family that fought off saboteurs with chow-chow and Johnny Cash.

Junior's tip jar overflowed. Ruby's livestream titled "Hargrove Balloon: Fireproof and McAllister-Proof" hit ten million views.

Reverend Potts showed up at lunch with a new sermon idea: "The Lord Protects Fools and Hot-Air Balloonists."

And somewhere in the treeline, a rustle of leaves sounded almost like tiny laughter.
The McAllisters had struck—and missed spectacularly.
Three days to launch.
The Hargroves were more united than ever.
And the Little People, apparently, were on the payroll.

Chapter 13:

Ruby's Viral Vortex, Tad's Tell-All Temptation, and Zeke's Kashehotapalo Prank

Thursday—the day before the big festival finale—dawned with a sky so blue it hurt to look at, the kind of Oklahoma weather that lulled you into thinking nothing could go wrong right before a tornado touched down.

The Hargrove pasture buzzed like a beehive on Red Bull. Final patches were sewn, the burner tested (and only singed Billy's eyebrows a little), and the basket loaded with sandbags for a full tethered lift later that afternoon. Crowds already gathered at the fence, phones up, waiting for the next installment of #HargroveChaos.

But inside the farmhouse kitchen, three grandkids were brewing storms of their own.

Ruby, sixteen and freshly minted social-media royalty, sat at the table scrolling her phone with the intensity of a stock trader during a crash. Her main account had hit two million followers overnight, thanks to the midnight McAllister raid clip titled "Okie Little People Roast Trespassers." Brands were sliding into her DMs: energy drinks, cowboy boots, even a laxative company (ironic, given the pie incident).

"Listen to this," she announced to the breakfast table, voice pitched with influencer excitement. "A talent agency in Tulsa wants to rep me. Says I could monetize the festival into a full series—'Dysfunctional Okies: Balloon or Bust.' They're offering ten grand up front and a cut of sponsorships."

Maude, flipping bacon, didn't look up. "Ten grand's nice, but fame's a fickle fart, sugar. One bad viral and you're yesterday's meme."

Darla, sipping coffee black enough to tar a roof, added, "And they'll want drama. More fights, more fires. You ready to sell your family for clicks?"

Ruby hesitated, thumb hovering over the reply button. "It's not selling. It's… documenting. Pa would've loved the attention."

Gertie, buttering biscuits, chuckled. "Earl loved attention like a hog loves mud. But he also hated bein' told what to do. That agency'll want scripted tears and fake feuds."

Billy, sketching burner tweaks on a napkin, mumbled, "As long as they don't touch the balloon."

Across the table, Tad—eighteen, quiet, and perpetually hunched over his notebook—scribbled furiously. He'd been writing nonstop since Gertie's arrival: family secrets, Earl's lows transcribed from old letters Gertie shared, even the moonshine hints Maude thought nobody noticed. The memoir was shaping into something raw—funny, painful, and potentially explosive.

Junior peeked over his shoulder. "Whatcha writin', nephew? Fan fiction?"
Tad slammed the notebook shut. "It's… a family history. For school."
Maude's eyes narrowed. "School don't assign three hundred pages on your grandpappy's bipolar antics and secret love child."

Tad flushed. "It's not for sale. Yet. But an editor DM'd me too—said if I finish it, they'd shop it to publishers. Advance could pay for college."

Darla set her mug down hard. "You're gonna air all our dirty overalls for strangers? Pa's bunker lows, Ma's resentment, my divorce—everything?"

Tad met her gaze, steady for once. "It's not gossip. It's honest. About how we survive the chaos. How the highs and lows don't break us—they make us Hargrove."

The kitchen went quiet except for bacon sizzling. Maude finally spoke. "Write what you need to, Tad. But remember: truth's a double-barreled shotgun. Hits the teller same as the told."

Before anyone could dig deeper, Zeke burst in from the porch, eyes wide as saucers, dragging a muddy stick twice his size.

"Y'all! The Kashehotapalo came last night! I saw it!"

The table erupted in groans and laughter. Gertie leaned forward. "The half-deer, half-man spirit? Choctaw folks say he guards the woods, scares bad hunters with woman-screams."

Zeke nodded vigorously. "I left extra cornbread for the Little People, as you said. Woke up at three 'cause I heard screamin'—like a lady in trouble! Ran outside and saw it: tall shadow with antlers, runnin' super-fast along the treeline. It looked right at me, then vanished!"

Billy perked up. "Could've been the McAllisters again, wearin' a deer head for camouflage."

Zeke shook his head. "No way. It moved wrong—too quick, too quiet. And it left this." He held up the stick. Carved into the bark were fresh scratches: symbols that looked suspiciously like Choctaw writing.

Maude took the stick, turning it over. "This ain't English. And it ain't prank-level carving."

Junior snapped a photo. "Postin' it. #KashehotapaloSighting. Views incoming."

Ruby was already filming Zeke's retelling for her story. "This is gold. Paranormal Okie folklore meets family feud!" Darla rubbed her temples. "Or it's Zeke pranking us for content."

Zeke looked wounded. "I swear on Pa's urn! I didn't carve it!"
Gertie studied the symbols, tracing them with a manicured nail. "My mama knew some Choctaw elders. This one means 'warning.' This one 'protect.' Looks like somethin' sayin', 'guard what's yours.'"

Maude handed the stick back to Zeke. "Then we listen. Double the watch tonight. And Zeke—no more midnight spirit-huntin' alone."
The morning dissolved into final preparations: envelope unfolded; burner ignited for the tethered test lift. The balloon rose beautifully—fifty feet,

steady, cowboy face beaming down like a proud patriarch.

Crowds cheered. Phones flashed. Ruby went live. Tad scribbled notes. Zeke stood guard with his carved stick like a tiny warrior.

But in the treeline, for just a second, a tall shadow flickered—antlers catching sunlight—before melting back into the woods.
Darla saw it this time. She didn't say a word, but her hand tightened on the shotgun.

Junior's phone buzzed with a new comment on the symbol photo: an account named @ChoctawStorykeeper wrote, "The old ones still walk when family fights for legacy. Respect the warning. Leave more cornbread."

Ruby read it aloud, voice hushed.
Billy laughed nervously. "Coincidence."

Maude looked at the balloon swaying gently overhead, then at her mismatched, magnificent family.

"Coincidence, spirit, or Zeke with too much sugar—don't matter. We've got one day left. Tomorrow, we fly, or we flop. Either way, we do it together."
She turned to the grandkids.
"Ruby, take your deals—but on your terms. Tad, write your truth—but show it to us first. Zeke… keep feedin' whatever's out there. Seems to like us."
Zeke grinned and saluted with the carved stick.
As the balloon tugged at its tethers, eager for open sky, a hot wind rustled the pasture grass.
Somewhere in it, faint as a whisper, came the sound of tiny footsteps—or maybe just laughter.
The Kashehotapalo was watching.
And tomorrow, the Hargroves would soar.

Chapter 14:

The Sheriff, the Still, and the Stolen Burner

Friday—the eve of the grand finale—started with the kind of perfect Oklahoma calm that always feels like the quiet before a twister drops out of a clear sky. The festival grounds were already swelling with out-of-towners: RVs parked bumper-to-bumper, food trucks slinging brisket and fried pie, and a news van from Tulsa setting up for the evening broadcast. Ruby's livestream counter ticked past fifteen million lifetime views. Junior had to empty his tip jar twice before lunch.

The balloon stood tethered in the pasture like a patient giant, envelope fully patched and gleaming in mismatched glory. Billy's Phoenix burner—Version 12.5, now with triple redundancies and a manual kill switch the size of a dinner plate—hummed through one last ground test. Everything, for once, worked.

Maude allowed herself a rare, full smile. "We might actually pull this off tomorrow."

Famous last words.

At 2:47 p.m., Sheriff Harlan Booth rolled up the driveway in his county cruiser, lights off but expression grim as a tax audit. Harlan was a lanky man with a mustache that had entered rooms before he did since 1987, and he'd known the Hargroves long enough to like them despite himself.

He climbed out, hooked thumbs in his belt, and nodded at Maude on the porch. "Afternoon, Maude. Hate to do this on festival eve, but I got a warrant."

Maude's smile evaporated. "Warrant for what? Noise complaint from the McAllisters again?"

Harlan pulled a folded paper from his pocket. "Search. An anonymous tip came in last night—said there's an illegal moonshine still on your property. ATF's breathin' down my neck. I gotta look."

The family, scattered across the yard on various tasks, froze mid-motion.

Darla dropped a coil of tether rope. "Anonymous tip? That's Clyde McAllister's handwriting all over it."

Billy's face went pale under his sunburn. "The still? But Pa buried that thing years ago…"

Maude shot him a look sharp enough to shave with. "William Hargrove, you knew about this?"

Billy shuffled. "Well… technically, it's still buried. Under the old bunker. Pa said it was 'retired.' I might've… checked on it last month. Just to make sure the copper wasn't tarnishin'."

Gertie whistled low. "Daddy always did love his side hustles."

Sheriff Booth sighed. "Maude, I don't want to tear up your land on festival weekend, but if there's an active still, I gotta confiscate it. Federal offense."

Maude pinched the bridge of her nose. "It ain't active. But it's there. Earl's folly, same as the balloon."

She led Harlan behind the barn to the bunker hatch, the family trailing like a funeral procession. Zeke clutched his carved Kashehotapalo stick for moral support.

The hatch creaked open to reveal concrete steps descending into cool darkness. Harlan's flashlight beam caught dust motes, shelves of canned goods, and Earl's old, scribbled blueprints still tacked to the walls.

At the back, behind a false panel Earl had built during one of his paranoid lows, sat the still: gleaming copper coils, oak barrels, and mason jars lined up like soldiers. A faint scent of mash and peach lingered in the air.

Harlan let out a low whistle. "Well, I'll be. That's the prettiest illegal rig I've seen since '09."

Billy stepped forward. "Sheriff, it's a historical artifact! Pa's legacy! Like the balloon!"

Harlan shook his head. "Legacy or not, it's evidence. I gotta call it in."

Maude's voice was steel. "Harlan Booth, you've eaten my peach cobbler every Fourth since you were knee-high. Give us till after the launch tomorrow. One flight for Earl. Then you can haul it away."

Harlan hesitated, mustache twitching. "Can't do that, Maude. Regulations."

That's when the second disaster struck.
Junior came running from the pasture, phone in one hand, panic in his eyes.

"The burner's gone! Somebody stole the whole Phoenix manifold—hoses, valves, the works!"
The family thundered back topside.
The tethered balloon still floated serenely, but the basket sat empty, burner rack stripped bare. Fresh tire tracks led from the pasture gate toward the McAllister boundary—wide, aggressive treads that screamed "dually pickup."

Darla cursed loud enough to scatter crows. "They waited till we were distracted with the sheriff."

Billy sank to his knees in the grass, manic energy crashing into despair. "Without that burner… we can't fly tomorrow. We lose the farm."

Gertie put a hand on his shoulder. "We'll build another."

"There's no time!" Billy's voice cracked. "Copper fittings, pressure gauges—we'd need a miracle."

Zeke tugged Maude's sleeve. "Maybe the Little People? Or Kashehotapalo? They warned us…"

Ruby, live-streaming the meltdown, had tears in her eyes for once. The chat scrolled with heartbroken emojis and offers of GoFundMe cash.

Sheriff Booth looked from the empty basket to the bunker, then at Maude's face—forty-five years of weathering Earl's storms etched in every line.

He exhaled through his mustache.

"Tell you what," he said quietly. "I'm gonna drive into town for… coffee. Takes me about an hour round-trip. If that still happens to vanish in the meantime—say, relocated to a spot I ain't searchin'—well, I can't confiscate what I don't find."

Maude met his eyes. "And the burner theft?"
Harlan tipped his hat. "I'll file the report. But investigatin' tire tracks across county lines… that could take days."

He climbed back into his cruiser and rolled away slowly, lights still off.
The family stared at the retreating dust cloud.
Junior broke the silence. "So… we movin' Pa's still tonight?"
Maude nodded once. "Every jar, coil, and barrel. We hide it where no warrant'll reach."

Darla cracked her knuckles. "And then we steal our burner back."

Gertie grinned like a Vegas hustler. "I know a thing or two about heists. Daddy taught me young."

Billy stood, despair flickering into something fiercer. "We fly tomorrow. No matter what." Zeke held up his carved stick. "I'll ask Kashehotapalo for help. Extra cornbread tonight."

From the treeline, a sudden flash of movement—tall shadow, antlers glinting—then gone.

Ruby's camera caught it. The livestream chat exploded: "GHOST?" "BIGFOOT?" "PROTECT THE HARGROVES!"

Maude looked at her family—singed, stubborn, and suddenly united in outlaw solidarity.

"Alright, you lunatics," she said. "We got a still to vanish and a burner to reclaim. Festival closes at midnight. We move under the cover of fireworks.

She turned toward the house, voice carrying the same steel that had survived forty-five years of Earl.

"One more folly for the road."

Tomorrow they would either soar higher than ever—or lose everything.
But tonight, the Hargroves were going rogue.

Chapter 15:

Midnight Moonshine Heist and the Burner Bandit Bust

Friday night settled over Weatherford like a velvet curtain, thick, dark, and perfect for mischief. The festival fireworks had just ended—red, white, and blue blooms fading over the midway—sending the last stragglers home with fried-food comas and souvenir foam acorns. By midnight, the only lights left were the Hargrove porch bulb and a half-moon peeking through scattered clouds.

Inside the farmhouse, the family gathered in the kitchen like outlaws planning a train heist. Maude had spread a hand-drawn map across the table: the farm, the bunker, the McAllister boundary, and two big X's—one for the still, one for the suspected burner hiding spot.

"Operation Double Folly," she declared. "Two teams. Team A: move the still. Team B: retrieve the burner. We rendezvous at the pond by 3 a.m. No lights, no phones except Junior's for emergencies, and nobody gets arrested."

Gertie, decked in black leggings and a dark hoodie that somehow still managed to sparkle, raised a hand. "I call Team B. Vegas taught me how to sneak into places I wasn't invited."

Darla cracked her knuckles. "I'm with Gertie. I owe the McAllisters for that laxative pie."

Billy, eyes bright with desperate invention, volunteered for Team A. "I know the still's plumbing best. If we gotta disassemble it quietly, I'm your man."

Junior and Tad also drew Team A—Junior for muscle, Tad for note-taking (he insisted it was "research"). Ruby and Zeke were on the bench, watching the porch with walkie-talkies made from old baby monitors.

Maude took Team A command. "Zeke, you keep that Kashehotapalo stick handy. And leave the biggest pile of cornbread yet on the stump. We need all the luck we can bribe."

Zeke saluted and scampered off to raid the kitchen.

By 12:30, both teams rolled out under the cover of darkness.

Team A: The Moonshine Vanish

Maude led Billy, Junior, and Tad down the bunker steps with red-filtered flashlights. The still gleamed accusingly in the dim glow—copper coils like a sleeping serpent, barrels labeled in Earl's scrawl: "Peach Lightning," "Scuppernong Surprise," "Bunker Blues Batch #9."

"Disassemble careful," Maude whispered. "Copper's soft—don't scratch it or it'll sing like a banjo."
They worked in practiced silence: Billy uncoupling joints, Junior hauling barrels up the steps one by one, Tad wrapping glass jars in old towels. Sweat soaked their shirts despite the cool night air.
Halfway through, Junior paused. "Y'all hear that?"
A faint rustle overhead—like tiny feet pattering across the hatch.
Billy froze. "Rats?"

Maude listened. The rustle stopped, then came a soft thump, as if something small had dropped onto the concrete outside.
They crept up the steps. On the ground beside the open hatch sat a fresh pile of acorns—perfectly stacked, like an offering returned.

Tad's eyes went wide. "Little People?"

Junior grinned in the dark. "Or Zeke playin' games." Maude picked up an acorn and rolled it between her fingers. "Either way, message received. Hurry up."

They finished in record time, loading the disassembled still into the bed of Junior's pickup, hidden under tarps and hay bales. By 2:15, the bunker looked innocent—just dusty shelves and Earl's old blueprints.

Team A rumbled off-road toward the pond, headlights off, guided by moonlight and memory.

Team B: The Burner Bandits

Gertie, Darla, and Reverend Potts (who'd shown up at midnight claiming "pastoral oversight of felonies") crept along the fence line separating Hargrove and McAllister land. Gertie had swapped her rhinestones for blackface greasepaint ("stage makeup—blends right in"), Darla carried bolt cutters and rock-salt shotgun, and Potts clutched his Bible like a getaway driver clutching the wheel.

They'd scouted earlier: the burner was almost certainly in Clyde McAllister's equipment shed, a big metal building lit by a single motion light.
Gertie took the point. "I'll distract. Darla cuts the padlock. Rev, you pray we don't get shot." Potts muttered, "Lord, forgive us our trespasses—and theirs for stealin' first."

Gertie sauntered toward the shed like she owned it, humming "9 to 5" loud enough to trigger the motion light. The door creaked open almost immediately—Clyde himself, in pajama pants and a shotgun. "Who's there?"

Gertie stepped into the light, hands up, a dazzling smile. "Evenin', sugar. Name's Gertie Lou. Heard you had somethin' belongs to my family. Thought we could negotiate like civilized folks." Clyde squinted, lowering the barrel a fraction. "You're Earl's… whatever. Get off my property."

While Clyde was distracted, Darla belly-crawled along the shed's shadow, snipping the padlock in three quiet bites. Potts whispered Psalms under his breath. Darla slipped inside. There it was: the Phoenix burner, sitting proudly on a workbench beside McAllister's tractor parts, still smelling of propane and victory.

She hefted it—awkward but manageable—and eased back out.

Gertie kept talking, voice honey-sweet. "Now, Clyde, we both know that burner's hot—literally and legally. Hand it over peacefully, nobody calls the sheriff about certain other items on your land." She nodded meaningfully toward Clyde's own suspiciously shiny copper coils visible through an open side door.

Clyde's face turned purple. "You threatenin' me?"
"Negotiatin'," Gertie corrected. "Big difference."

Darla emerged behind Clyde; burner cradled like a baby. She gave Gertie a thumbs-up. Gertie winked.
"Looks like we're done here. Night, handsome."
They backed away slow, then bolted for the fence. Clyde's roar followed them into the dark, along with a shotgun blast into the air—warning, not aim.

Team B sprinted across the pasture, laughing breathlessly, burner intact.

Rendezvous at the Pond

Both teams converged at the pond by 3 a.m., moon silvering the water. The still parts were already submerged in a waterproof crate anchored deep—Earl's old "treasure" spot, now repurposed. The burner sat ready for reinstallation.

Maude surveyed her ragtag crew—sweaty, triumphant, and utterly unrepentant.
"We did it," Darla whispered, half disbelieving.

Billy hugged the burner manifold like a long-lost child. "Tomorrow, we fly."

Gertie flopped onto the grass, staring at the stars. "Daddy would've been proud. Illegal, insane, and unbeatable."

Reverend Potts, panting, added, "And possibly forgivable."

Zeke appeared from the shadows, carved stick in hand. "The cornbread's gone. All of it. And look—" He pointed to the stump. The empty plate now held a single perfect arrowhead, flint knapped sharp and new.

Tad picked it up reverently. "Choctaw style. Old ones."

Junior snapped a photo. "Proof."

Maude took the arrowhead, tucked it into her pocket. "Proof we've got friends in low places—and maybe high ones too."

She looked at the family circled in moonlight, then at the dark silhouette of the balloon waiting in the pasture.

"Get some sleep. Dawn comes early. Tomorrow, we finish what Earl started." As they trudged home, a faint rustle followed them through the grass—tiny footsteps keeping pace, then fading.
The Little People—or something older—were walking them home.
One day left.
The balloon would rise.
And the Hargroves, against all odds and several laws, were ready.

Chapter 16:

Launch Day Lightning and the Low-Point Lament

Saturday—the grand finale of Pa's Folly Festival—dawned hotter than the devil's anvil and twice as mean. By 8 a.m., the mercury was pushing ninety-five, humidity thick enough to chew, and the sky hung low and bruised like it was spoiling for a fight. Oklahoma summer at its finest: beautiful, brutal, and unpredictable.

The midway was already a madhouse. Record crowds—five thousand strong, according to the sheriff's estimate—filled the grounds: families in lawn chairs, news crews from Tulsa and OKC, food vendors serving ice-cold lemonade like it was liquid gold, and Ruby's livestream soaring at twenty million views worldwide. Junior's tip jar had been replaced by a five-gallon bucket. Zeke patroled the perimeter with his carved Kashehotapalo stick like a pint-sized sentinel.

In the pasture, the balloon stood ready: envelope pristine (well, as pristine as a junkyard Frankenstein could be), basket loaded with sandbags for ballast, the reclaimed Phoenix burner gleaming in the morning sun. Tethers held it gently aloft in a cold inflate, cowboy face beaming down on the family like Earl himself giving a thumbs-up.

Maude stood at the fence line in her best denim dress, arms crossed, surveying the scene with the grim satisfaction of a general before battle.
"We launch at four," she announced to the assembled crew. "Wind's supposed to stay light till sunset. Gives the crowd a show, us a safe flight, and the McAllisters one last chance to behave."

Billy, buzzing on coffee and adrenaline, checked gauges for the tenth time. "Pressure perfect. Fuel load optimal. We'll hit two hundred feet easy, circle the farm, land soft as a kiss."

Darla eyed the darkening western sky. "Weather app says scattered storms after six. We'll be down by then."

Gertie tuned her karaoke machine for the pre-launch playlist—Earl's favorites only. Reverend Potts milled about offering blessings and accepting free brisket.

The grandkids were everywhere: Ruby live-streaming interviews, Tad scribbling final chapters, Zeke leaving one last massive cornbread offering on the stump with a note scrawled in crayon: "Thank you for the help. Please no tornado today."

Everything was perfect.

Until it wasn't.

At 2:45 p.m.—ninety minutes to launch—the wind shifted.
It came suddenly and sharply from the west, carrying the smell of rain and electricity. Clouds boiled up like ink in water. The temperature dropped ten degrees in minutes. Festival flags snapped taut. Porta-potties rocked on their bases.

The National Weather Service siren wailed from town: severe thunderstorm warning, possible rotation, hail, sixty-mile-an-hour gusts.

Crowds murmured, then panicked. Parents scooped up the kids. Vendors battened hatches. The news crews pivoted to storm coverage.

Maude stared at the sky, jaw tight. Billy's face crumpled. "We can't launch in this. Gusts'll rip the envelope like tissue." Darla checked her phone. "Storm's supposed to blow through by five, but the front behind it brings worse. We'd have maybe thirty minutes of clear before round two."
Junior kicked the dirt. "We miss the window; we miss the deadline. Will says launch at the festival finale. Finale's tonight."

Gertie looked at the deflating envelope—literally sagging as wind buffeted the tethers—and then at Maude.

"We lose the farm," she said quietly. "All this for nothing."
The family gathered in a loose circle, the weight of it settling like wet wool.

Billy sank to the grass, manic spark gone cold. "I failed him. Pa's balloon, Pa's dream—grounded by weather. Just like everything else I touch."

Darla's eyes filled, anger turning inward. "I should've sabotaged the McAllisters harder. Or never come back from Tulsa. I'm the one with sense, and I still let us get this far."

Tad closed his notebook. "The book ends with failure. Great legacy."

Ruby ended her livestream for the first time all week, tears streaking her makeup. "I hyped it to millions. Now I tell them we quit?"

Even Zeke's lip trembled. "Kashehotapalo didn't stop the storm. Maybe Pa's ghost is mad at us." Reverend Potts tried a prayer, but it died in the rising wind.

Maude stood silent longest, staring at the balloon whipping against its ropes. Forty-five years of Earl's highs and lows flashed behind her eyes: the drive-thru chapel, the squirrel siege, the bunker nights when he'd cry into her lap, the mornings he'd wake convinced he could fly.

She felt the old resentment rise—then something else. Love, stubborn and fierce. "No," she said finally, voice cutting through the wind. "We ain't quittin'."

Everyone turned.

Maude stepped forward, grabbed a loose tether rope that was whipping around, and hauled it hand-over-hand until the envelope steadied.
"We launch now," she said. "Right now. Storm's still twenty miles west. We go up quick, short flight—ten, fifteen minutes—circle once, land before the front hits. It's risky, but it's flying. Will says, 'launch at the festival finale.' Finale's whenever we say it is."
Billy blinked. "But the crowd's scattering—"
"Then we fly for us," Maude snapped. "For Earl. Not for cameras or bets or likes. Cut the cold air fans. Fire the burner. We go light—no sandbags, minimal fuel. Just family."

Gertie grinned first—a slow, Vegas-bright smile. "Hell yes."

Darla nodded, wiping her eyes. "I'm in."

Billy jumped up, spark reigniting. "Light crew only! Me, Maude, Gertie, Darla—four bodies max for lift. Junior handles ground crew with the kids."

Junior saluted. "We'll guide tethers till you're clear, then reel you in fast on landing."

Ruby restarted her stream, voice steady now. "Emergency launch, y'all. This one's for Pa."

Tad opened his notebook again. "This ending's better."

Zeke ran to the stump, grabbed the empty cornbread plate, and yelled toward the treeline, "We're flying! Wish us luck!"

They worked like a machine born for this moment: burner reinstalled in minutes, tethers adjusted, basket cleared. The remaining crowd—those brave or crazy enough to stay—cheered as the envelope filled with hot air, rising defiant against the darkening sky.

Lightning flickered far west. Thunder rumbled like distant applause.
At 3:15 p.m., with winds gusting but still manageable, Maude climbed into the basket first.
Then Gertie, Darla, Billy.
Junior and the grandkids held the crown line.
Reverend Potts offered one last blessing: "Lord, hold the storm back ten minutes. That's all we ask."
Maude looked at her children—blood and chosen—then at the ground crew.

"On three," she said. "One… two… three—release!"

Tethers dropped. The balloon surged upward, fast and free.
They cleared the treetops in seconds, wind catching them, pushing east ahead of the storm. From the basket, Weatherford spread below like a patchwork

quilt: the festival shrinking, the farm tiny and perfect, the pond glinting.

Lightning flashed again—closer now.
But for one shining moment, they were flying.
Earl's balloon, built from junk and held together by folly, soared at last.
And the Hargroves—highs, lows, secrets, and all—were exactly where they belonged.

Chapter 17:

Storm Riders and the Secret of the Will

The balloon climbed fast—too fast. The storm wind at ground level had been a breeze; up here, two hundred feet and rising, it was a living thing, shoving them eastward like a bully with a grudge.

Maude gripped the basket rim, knuckles white. "Billy, throttle down! We're gainin' altitude quicker than a lie in church."

Billy twisted the burner valve, flame dropping to a steady blue roar. "We're light—no ballast. Storm's pushin' us. Good news: we're flyin'. Bad news: we're flyin' toward the thunderheads."

Darla peered over the edge, hair whipping across her face. "Farm's already half a mile back. Pond looks like a nickel down there."

Gertie laughed—wild, exhilarated, pure Earl. "Look at it! All of Weatherford spread out like God's own checkerboard. Daddy's seein' this, I know he is."

Lightning forked across the western sky, illuminating the underside of the clouds in electric purple. Thunder followed seconds later, deep and rolling. Below, the ground crew—Junior, the grandkids, Reverend Potts, and a few hundred stubborn spectators—watched the balloon shrink against the darkening horizon. Ruby's livestream chat scrolled frantic: "They're gonna die!" "This is epic!" "Prayers up!"

Inside the basket, the mood swung between terror and triumph.
Billy's eyes darted to the gauges. "Fuel's burnin' faster than planned. Wind's cold up here—hot air coolin' quick. We got maybe twelve minutes before we start droppin'."

Maude scanned the landscape. Open pastures gave way to wooded hills, then the wide bend of the Canadian River. "We need a landing spot east of the storm track. Clear field, no power lines."

Darla pointed southeast. "There—McAllister's north pasture. Flat, fenced, nothin' but cows."

Gertie snorted. "Land on Clyde's land? He'll shoot us down for trespassin'."

Maude's jaw set. "Better shot at than struck by lightning. Billy, vent some air. Start descent."

Billy yanked the vent line. Hot air whooshed out the top, and the balloon began to sink—slow at first, then faster as a downdraft caught them.

Rain started as a mist, then needles. Wind howled through the rigging. The basket rocked like a cradle in a hurricane.

Gertie grabbed Maude's hand. "If we don't make it, I just want you to know—I'm glad I came. Glad I got to be family, even for a week."

Maude squeezed back, eyes fierce. "We're makin' it. Hargroves don't die dramatic—we live ridiculous."

Darla laughed through chattering teeth. "Speak for yourself. I'm freezin' my roots off."

Lightning struck close—close enough to raise the hair on their arms. Thunder cracked overhead like the sky splitting.

The balloon dropped hard, stomach-lurching. Below, McAllister pasture rushed up fast: green grass, scattered cows, a single windmill spinning wildly.

Billy blasted the burner one last time for cushion. "Brace!"

The basket hit with a bone-jarring thud, skidded twenty yards through mud and cow patties, then tipped sideways. Ropes tangled. The envelope deflated overhead like a giant sigh. Silence—broken only by rain drumming on nylon and distant thunder retreating east.

They climbed out soaked, bruised, and very much alive.

Cows stared at them, chewing cud like unimpressed critics.

Gertie flopped onto her back in the mud, laughing hysterically. "We did it! We flew the fool thing!"

Darla joined her, then Billy. Even Maude allowed herself a muddy grin.

Headlights approached—two pickups roaring across the field. Clyde McAllister and his twins, shotguns in hand.

Clyde stepped out, face thunderous. "You got some nerve crashin' on my"
He stopped. Saw the deflated balloon, the soaked Hargroves covered in mud and glory, and something in his expression shifted. Maybe it was the sheer absurdity. Maybe it was the echo of Earl he saw in their faces.
He lowered the shotgun.

"You flew it," he said, almost accusing.
Maude stood, dripping. "We did. Short flight, but it counts. Will's satisfied."
Clyde stared a long moment, then spat in the mud. "Earl was crazier than a sack of cats. Guess it runs in the family."

He turned to his sons. "Help 'em load the basket. Storm's comin' back around." The twins blinked, but obeyed—hauling ropes, folding nylon alongside Hargroves without a word.

By the time they got everything onto Clyde's flatbed, the rain had eased to a drizzle. The western sky cleared just enough for a rainbow to arc over the farm in the distance—bright, ridiculous, perfect.

Back at the festival grounds—now mostly empty, muddy, and littered with blown-over chairs—the family gathered one last time under the main stage awning.

Junior had saved the announcement mic. Ruby's livestream, somehow still running on cellular, showed half a million viewers watching the aftermath. Maude climbed the steps, took the mic, and pulled the will from her apron pocket—miraculously dry inside a Ziploc Darla had insisted on.

"Y'all stuck around through fire, flood, and folly," she said, voice carrying over the speakers. "We flew

Earl's balloon. Didn't go far, didn't go pretty, but we went up. And we came down together."

Cheers rose—wet, weary, but genuine.

Maude unfolded the will, held it up.

"But here's the part Earl never told us. The real secret."

She read aloud the final paragraph none of them had noticed in the armadillo chaos:

"'To my beloved pack of fools: The balloon ain't about winnin'. It's about remindin' you that highs and lows both lift you if you share the basket. The farm don't go to one—it stays with all. Together, or not at all. Now quit fightin' and eat some pie.'"

Silence. Then Gertie started laughing. Darla joined. Billy whooped. The grandkids tackled Maude in a muddy group hug.

Clyde McAllister, standing at the back with his twins, actually cracked a smile.

Reverend Potts raised his Bible. "Amen and hallelujah."

Junior hit play on the karaoke machine. "Cluckin' Heartbreak Blues" filled the night one last time. The family sang—off-key, soaked, exhausted, and whole.

Above them, the rainbow faded, but a single bright star winked on—like Earl tipping his hat.

The balloon lay folded in the mud, torn and triumphant.
The farm was safe.

And the Hargroves—manic, depressive, secret-filled, and stubbornly loving—were finally, truly flying.

Chapter 18:

Rainbow Reckonings and the Reverend's Redemption Pie

The storm had blown itself out by midnight, leaving the festival grounds a glorious mess of mud puddles, overturned chairs, and rainbow light glinting off scattered foam acorns. A cleanup crew of volunteers—mostly locals who'd stayed for the drama—worked under portable floodlights, hauling trash and righting booths while trading exaggerated tales of the Hargrove flight.

On the main stage, the family sat in a semicircle of mismatched lawn chairs, too wired to go home, too tired to move. The deflated balloon lay heaped nearby like a conquered dragon, cowboy face mud-streaked but still grinning.

Maude held the will in her lap, tracing Earl's scrawl with one finger. The Ziploc had kept it dry; the words inside had finally set them free.
Darla broke the quiet first. "So, the whole competition thing… was just Pa's way of herdin' cats. Typical."

Gertie nodded, boots propped on an overturned cooler. "He knew we'd fight tooth and nail if there was a prize. But fight together if the prize was each other."

Billy, wrapped in a blanket despite the lingering humidity, managed a sheepish smile. "I was ready to kill for that deed. Feels stupid now."

Maude looked at him—really looked. "You swung high and low this week, same as your daddy. But you kept swingin'. That ain't stupid. That's Hargrove."

Reverend Potts arrived carrying a pie tin balanced on his Bible like an offering. Steam rose from a perfect lattice crust.

"Mrs. Potts heard about the crash landin'," he announced. "Sent her famous peach redemption pie. Said even outlaws deserve dessert."

He set it on a folding table someone had salvaged. The smell—sweet, buttery, with a hint of cinnamon—drew the grandkids like moths.

Ruby cut the first slice, handing it to Maude. "For the captain."

Maude took it, fork pausing midway. "I spent years resentful—cleanin' up Earl's messes, holdin' the farm together while he chased rainbows. Thought I deserved better than chaos."

She took a bite, eyes closing. "But this week… chaos brought Gertie home. Made Billy ask for help instead of hiding his lows. Got Darla to stay longer than a weekend. Turned Junior's laziness into a business empire. Gave the kids stories they'll tell their own kids."

She looked around the circle. "Turns out the mess was the better thing all along."

Darla accepted her slice next. "I came home plannin' to fix y'all. Left knowin' I was the one needin' fixin'. I'm movin' back from Tulsa. Openin' a salon right here in Weatherford. Callin' it 'Folly Cuts.'"
Cheers and hugs erupted.

Gertie raised her plastic cup of scuppernong (salvaged from the bunker before its midnight relocation). "I'm splittin' time—Vegas gigs in winter, Oklahoma summers. Got a stand-up routine brewin':

'Raised by a Secret Okie.' Already booked my first slot."

Billy cleared his throat. "I'm startin' therapy. Real one, not Reverend Potts's pasture version." He glanced at Potts. "No offense."
Potts waved a fork. "None taken. My methods are… unconventional."

Junior checked his phone. "Museum expansion's funded—tips, merch, and a GoFundMe Ruby set up. Gonna call the new wing 'Earl's Folly Flight.' Balloon goes on permanent display, mud stains and all."

Ruby grinned. "Agency deal's signed, but on my terms—no scripted drama. Just real life. Season Two starts with salon opening."

Tad handed Maude a printed page—title sheet of his manuscript. "Finished it tonight. Callin' it Highs, Lows, and Hot Air: A Hargrove Legacy. Dedication reads: 'To the family that taught me crazy can be kind.'"

Zeke, face sticky with peach, held up his carved stick. "And I'm gonna be a storyteller. Like the Choctaw elders. Kashehotapalo and the Little People helped us—I'm gonna keep leavin' cornbread so they stick around."

Maude ruffled his hair. "Just not in my kitchen."

A comfortable quiet settled, broken only by forks scraping tin and distant crickets starting their night chorus.

Then headlights swept the grounds—Clyde McAllister's pickup, pulling a flatbed with the folded balloon basket. He climbed out, twins trailing like reluctant shadows. Clyde cleared his throat. "Figured y'all'd need this back. Saved us a trip tomorrow."

Maude stood. "Appreciate it, Clyde."

He shuffled, eyes on his boots. "Heard the will's real meanin'. Earl... he wasn't all bad. Used to help my daddy fix tractors durin' his highs. Never charged a dime."

He reached into the cab, pulled out a second pie tin. "My wife's cherry. Not poisoned this time."

Laughter rippled—tension finally snapping like an old rubber band.
Clyde extended a hand to Maude. "Truce?"
Maude shook it firm. "Truce. Long as you keep your cows outta my north pasture."
"Deal."

The McAllisters stayed for pie. By the time the tins were empty, stories flowed both directions—Earl's antics, Clyde's daddy's moonshine mishaps, shared history neither family had acknowledged in years.
As the floodlights dimmed and stars reclaimed the sky, the Hargroves walked home together across the muddy field.

The balloon stayed behind—destined for Junior's museum—but its shadow lingered in their steps:

lighter now, shared. Maude paused at the porch, looking back at the festival grounds one last time. "Earl," she whispered to the night, "you old fool. You got your flight. And you got us talkin'. Hope you're happy."

A warm breeze rustled the pecan trees—almost like laughter.
Inside, the family scattered to showers and beds, voices echoing through open windows: plans, jokes, the easy rhythm of people who'd survived themselves.

The farm was safe.

The legacy wasn't land or copper stills or even a junkyard balloon.
It was them—messy, manic, mended, and moving forward together.
And somewhere in the treeline, tiny footsteps faded into the dark, cornbread plate empty, arrowhead left in thanks.

The Little People were content.

So were the Hargroves.

Chapter 19: The Still's Final Resting Place and the Sheriff's Second Visit

Sunday morning broke gentle over Weatherford, the kind of soft, golden light that made Saturday's storm feel like a tall tale. The festival grounds were mostly cleared—booths dismantled, trash hauled, only a few mud puddles and trampled grass left as evidence of the chaos. Word had spread overnight: the Hargroves had flown, crashed, and somehow won anyway. Church attendance was up; Reverend Potts's sermon on "Grace in Gusts" was standing-room only.

At the farm, the family slept late for the first time all week. Maude rose first, brewed coffee strong enough to wake the dead, and stepped onto the porch with a mug and Earl's old arrowhead from the Little People. She turned it over in her palm, feeling its smooth edges.

"Old fool," she murmured to the morning. "You got more than you bargained for."

Footsteps crunched gravel. Sheriff Harlan Booth's cruiser rolled up slow, no lights, no hurry. He climbed out carrying a paper sack from the diner and that same mustache that had seen everything twice.

"Mornin', Maude." He tipped his hat. "Brought breakfast burritos. Figured y'all earned 'em."

Maude eyed him. "You here to arrest us for the still relocation?"

Harlan handed over the sack. "Officially? I searched the bunker yesterday and found nothin' but dust and mouse turds. Report's filed. Case closed."

He paused, leaning on the porch rail. "Unofficially… I drove by the pond at dawn. Saw fresh tire tracks and a crate-shaped disturbance in the mud. Reckon whatever was down there is now deeper than my jurisdiction."

Maude sipped her coffee. "Reckon so."

Harlan nodded toward the pasture, where the balloon basket sat waiting for Junior's museum trailer. "Heard you flew it. Short, but flew."

"We did."

He scratched his mustache. "Earl would've whooped like a banshee."

Maude smiled—small, real. "He did. Somewhere."

Harlan shifted. "About that still… copper that fine deserves better than rustin' at the bottom of a pond. If somebody was to fish it out quiet-like, clean it up, and donate it to, say, the Choctaw Nation cultural center in Tuskahoma—they got a moonshine exhibit, educational purposes only—I might could look the other way on transport."

Maude raised an eyebrow. "Educational purposes?"

"History of prohibition-era ingenuity in Oklahoma. Fits right in with Choctaw resilience stories." He shrugged. "Just a thought."

Maude considered, then extended her hand. "Deal. On one condition—you help us haul it up tonight. Your truck's got a winch."

Harlan shook on it. "Fair enough."

The screen door creaked. Gertie emerged in pajamas and cowboy boots, hair a glorious mess. "Did I hear somebody sayin', 'haul the still'? I call shotgun."

Darla followed, yawning. "If we're divin' for copper, I want pancakes first."

Billy wandered out last, eyes clearer than they'd been in weeks. "I'll sketch a proper cradle, so we don't scratch it. Museum-grade recovery."

By evening, under a sky full of stars and no threat of storm, the operation went smooth as greased bacon. Harlan's winch pulled the waterproof crate from the pond depths like Excalibur from the lake. Water lilies and a curious catfish came up with it.

They rinsed the still under the garden hose—copper gleaming like new in the porch light. Even Harlan whistled.

"Finest rig I never saw," he said.

Junior snapped photos for the museum's "anonymous donor" plaque. Zeke left one final slice of cornbread on the crate lid "for the water spirits." Gertie ran a finger along the coils. "Daddy's masterpiece. Goin' to a place that'll tell his story right—no shame, just survival."

Maude wrapped it in quilts for transport. "He'd like that. Choctaw blood on both sides of the family, way back. Full circle."

Harlan and Billy loaded it into the sheriff's locked trailer—headed for Tuskahoma come morning. Before he left, Harlan paused. "Y'all turned out okay, Maude. Earl too, in his way."

Maude watched the taillights disappear down the county road.

Inside, the family gathered one last time in the kitchen—no pie this time, just leftover brisket sandwiches and sweet tea. They talked quiet: plans, dreams, the ordinary magic of a future without a deadline.

Darla toasted with her glass. "To Pa's folly."

"To family," Gertie added.

"To flying," Billy said.

"To cornbread offerings," Zeke chimed.

Maude raised her tea last. "To all of it. Highs, lows, and the hot air in between."

They clinked glasses, laughter soft and easy. Outside, a gentle breeze moved through the pecan trees. If you listened carefully, you might hear tiny footsteps slipping away into the woods—satisfied, mission accomplished.

The still was gone to its honorable retirement.
The balloon was headed for display.
The farm—and the family—were home to stay.

Epilog Chapter 20:

One Year Later – The Calmer Folly

The first Saturday in June dawned hot and clear, same as always, but the Pa's Folly Festival looked different now. Bigger, polished around the edges, yet still unmistakably Hargrove.

A new arched sign spanned the entrance gate: **PA'S FOLLY FESTIVAL – EST. IN MEMORY OF EARL HARGROVE, WHO TAUGHT US TO FLY ANYWAY**. Below it, a bronze plaque read: "Highs, lows, and hot air: the family glue."

Junior's roadside museum—now a proper building with air-conditioning and actual doors—drew steady crowds. The star exhibit was the balloon itself, hanging from the rafters like a triumphant battle flag:

patched, mud-stained, cowboy face restored and grinning eternally. Beside it, Earl's copper still gleamed under glass in the new "Oklahoma Ingenuity Wing," on permanent loan from the Choctaw Cultural Center with a discreet plaque: "Anonymous gift of the Hargrove Family – May it educate, not intoxicate."

Darla's salon, Folly Cuts, occupied the old barn loft—shiplap walls, vintage dryers, and a neon sign that read "Bad Hair Days Welcome." On festival days she offered "Earl's Manic Special": wild colors and zero judgment.

Ruby's channel had exploded into a full media brand—Okie Chaos Chronicles—with a crew, sponsors, and a podcast recorded right from the farmhouse porch. She still lived at home, saving for film school, but her live streams now funded college scholarships for Weatherford kids.

Tad's book, Highs, Lows, and Hot Air, sat on the New York Times regional bestseller list for six months straight. He was a sophomore at OSU now, majoring in creative writing, but home every weekend to sign copies in the museum gift shop.

Zeke, thirteen and still feral, led "Little People Tours" through the woods—complete with cornbread offerings and stories of Kashehotapalo sightings that may or may not have been embellished. The stump always had fresh crumbs by morning.

Billy had good days and hard days, but the hard ones no longer swallowed him whole. Therapy, medication tweaks, and a part-time job welding museum display kept him steady. His latest invention—a solar-powered funnel-cake fryer—was the festival's biggest hit.

Gertie split her year clean down the middle: winter headlining a Vegas revue, summer in Weatherford with family. Her stand-up set "Secret Okie Daughter" sold out every show, but she always flew home for festival week.

And Maude—Maude was still the center. She'd turned the north pasture into a community garden, taught taxidermy classes in the barn (ethical only, from roadkill), and become the unofficial matriarch of half the county.

The festival itself had grown, but not too much. Same bluegrass stage, same pie contests (McAllisters took blue ribbon in cherry this year—no laxatives), same parade down Airport Road. Only now, the grand marshal float was a flatbed carrying the original balloon basket, pulled by Clyde McAllister's restored '78 Ford. Clyde waved from the driver's seat like it was the most natural thing in the world.

At dusk, the family gathered in the back pasture—the exact spot where the balloon had risen and fallen a year ago. A new tradition: a tethered hot-air balloon ride, this time professionally operated, safe and insured, offering short hops over the farm at sunset.

But tonight, the basket held only Hargroves. Maude climbed in first, then the rest—Darla, Billy, Gertie, Junior, the grandkids. Plenty of room now; no need to fly light.

The burner burned steadily and softly. The envelope—new, bright, professionally made, but painted with the old cowboy face—lifted them smoothly and easily into the golden evening.

From two hundred feet, Weatherford spread out peacefully and small: the festival lights twinkling on below, the pond catching the last rays, the woods dark and deep where tiny footsteps sometimes walked.

Zeke pointed. "Look—cornbread's gone already."
Ruby filmed it all, but quietly this time—no commentary, just family.
Darla leaned on the rim beside Maude. "Think Pa's watchin'?"

Maude smiled, eyes on the horizon where the sun bled orange and pink.

"He is. Took him long enough to get us all in one basket."

Gertie started humming "Cluckin' Heartbreak Blues." One by one, the others joined—soft, off-key, perfect.

The balloon drifted lazy circles over the farm, wind calm, sky vast.

Below, the festival carried on—laughter, music, the smell of brisket and fried dough rising like incense.

Above, the Hargroves floated together scarred, healed, whole.

Highs and lows still came, same as Oklahoma weather.

But now they rode them side by side.

And each year, on the first Saturday in June, they rose again—just high enough to remember what it felt like to fly.

The End

Made in the USA
Coppell, TX
21 January 2026

68879956R00095